SANDS *of* TIME

Following in
the footsteps of
CEDRIC
ROBINSON
on
MORECAMBE BAY

LINDSAY SUTTON

GREAT-N-ORTHERN

*In memory of my brother Graham,
with gratitude to my wife Mo,
and grateful thanks to John Holland.*

(Picture by Paul Nickson)

Great Northern Books Limited
PO Box 1380, Bradford, BD5 5FB
www.greatnorthernbooks.co.uk

ISBN: 978-1-912101-10-8

Design and layout: David Burrill

CIP Data
A catalogue for this book is available from the British
Library

Cover illustration: Paul Nickson

Endpaper illustration:
ALL CHANGE: Morecambe Bay, its channels, its
fishing grounds, and the routes of the cross-bay
walks (dotted lines), as they were laid out decades
ago before the reconfiguration of the sands.
(Drawing by Olive Robinson)

Contents

Forewords

Cedric Robinson holds a special place in the hearts and memories of the thousands of people he has guided safely across the sands of Morecambe Bay, a beautiful but hazardous stretch of tempting sands at low tide.

He has won national recognition for his skill and knowledge and has, for a record 55 years, held a special position as Queen's Guide to Morecambe Bay, for which he was awarded the MBE. On one notable occasion, he guided HRH The Duke of Edinburgh across the Bay by horse and carriage, an event enjoyed by all.

Many charities have reason to be grateful to Cedric. His regular guided, cross-bay walks for hardy fundraisers have raised many thousands of pounds for good causes.

This book focuses on his remarkable relationship with Morecambe Bay. It is testament to a man whose service has been legendary. In company with countless others, I wish him well, hoping that he has managed to pass on some of his invaluable knowledge to his successor.

HM Lord-Lieutenant of Cumbria
Mrs Claire Hensman

It is not often in the age of the hustle, bustle and tumble of British politics that something comes across our desks here in this House which unites our thoughts and beliefs. News that the Queen's Guide to Morecambe Bay, Cedric Robinson MBE, is to be engaged in a new position after serving over 55 years as Her Majesty's Guide, certainly has united us.

I'm delighted to acknowledge the immense contribution and dedication Cedric has made since his original appointment in 1963.

He has helped hundreds of charities and other similar organisations, both large and small. Not just from within my constituency, but from all over the North West and beyond, leading thousands of walkers safely across Morecambe Bay as they follow his footprints in the sand.

These walkers have in turn raised hundreds of thousands of pounds to help support vital services that so many have need of today, whilst getting to experience the wonders and natural beauty that is Morecambe Bay.

I wish Cedric much success in his new Advisory and Ambassadorial appointment to the Duchy of Lancaster and place on record my sincere thanks and gratitude for what he has done for so many and for so long. I also congratulate his replacement Guide, Michael Wilson, as he takes over the mantle and responsibility.

Cedric is most probably one of the Queen's longest-serving servants, if not the longest. His determination to continue this lifetime of dedication and commitment is an example to us all.

So once again on behalf of everyone you have helped, I thank you.

The Rt Hon
Sir Lindsay Hoyle
MP
Deputy Speaker,
House of Commons

(Oil on board by
Liam Dickinson)

List of Guides to the Kent Sands from Henry VIII onwards in the 1530s

1501	Edmondson	*[Edward Barbour]* *Not certain to have been a guide.* *'Carter upon Kent Sands'*
Before 1535-?	William Gate	*Mentioned in the Valor Ecclesiasticus.* *Paid by the Prior of Cartmel.*
1538-?	Thomas Hogeson	*Appointed by Letters Patent dated 8th February* *1538 and reappointed on 29th January 1548.*
?-1564	Richard Carter	*Burial entry dated 20th March 1564.*
1564-1592	William Carter	*Known to have succeeded Richard Carter,* *and to have been buried in 1592.*
1592-[1602]	William Carter	*Will proven at Richmond in 1602.*
1602-1633	Edward Carter	
1633-1644	Edward Carter	*Burial entry in Cartmel register,* *dated 14th December 1644.*
1644-1649	William Carter	*Will proven at Richmond in 1649.*
1649-1661	Thomas Carter	*Will proven at Richmond in 1661.*
1661-1672	William Carter	*Will proven at Richmond in 1672.*
1672-1698	John Carter	*Drowned in 1698, in the course of his duty.*
1698-1718	John Carter	*Who petitioned for an increase in salary.*
1718-1728	?	
1728-1745	John Carter	*Appointed by Letters Patent dated 23rd March 1728.*
[?1745]-1759	Edward Carter	*Buried 23rd March 1759. Will proven in 1759.*
1759-[?1787]	John Carter	*Record of payment in 1775.*
1787-[?1800]	William Carter	*Appointed by Letters Patent dated 9th February 1787.*
[1800-1828]	William Carter	
1828-[1856]	James Carter	*Appointed on 8th August 1828.*
[1856-1867]	James 'John' Carter	*James Carter the younger? Census return for 1861.*
1867-1873	John Nevison	*Appointed on 10th December 1867 and later dismissed.*
1873-1919	George Sedgwick	*Appointed on 28th August 1873.*
1919-1943	John (Jack) Burrow	*Appointed 14th February 1919.*
1943-1950	John (Jack) R D Burrow	*Appointed on 5th August 1943. Died in early 1950,* *after having resigned. The son of the former guide.*
1950-1963	William Burrow	*Appointed on 12th January 1950.* *Died in office in 1963.*
1963-2019	Cedric Robinson MBE	*Appointed on 1st October 1963. The position* *changed after over 55 years to that of an* *Ambassadorial and Advisory role on the 25th* *January 2019.*
2019	Michael Wilson	*Appointed on 25th January 2019.*

Base information provided by Dr Terry Marsh, MA (Lake District Studies); PhD (Historical Geography); FRGS; FSA (Scot); *Plus,* **details from the book,** *Cedric Robinson: 40 Years on Morecambe Bay,* **published in 2003 and updated in January 2019.**

Lives of great men all remind us

We can make our lives sublime.

And, departing, leave behind us

Footprints on the sands of time.

Henry Wadsworth Longfellow

Introduction

CEDRIC Robinson needs little introduction, but he does need a big pat on the back for all that he has achieved as the record-breaking Queen's Guide to the Sands in Morecambe Bay.

Thousands of people throughout the country, and even overseas, know of Cedric, through his legendary cross-bay walks and his help in guiding thousands of charity fundraisers through the channels and around the often treacherous quicksands.

Now, as he hands on the baton, and takes on a transitional role as 'Ambassador of the Sands' and advisor to the incoming Guide, this book aims to be more than a fulsome celebration of Cedric's achievements. Naturally, it celebrates his record-breaking 55 years as the longest-serving Guide to the nation's longest-serving monarch. It also reflects his warmth, his basic charm, his character, and his often-wicked sense of humour. However, the book aims to look well beyond his well-chronicled role. It looks at what has happened, and what is currently happening, to the Bay and its surrounding communities, through the prism of Cedric's long tenure as a 'Man of the Sands.'

From climate change to social change; from changes to the channels, the sands, and the coastline; from changes in the wildlife – in and out of the water; to the changing face of Morecambe Bay itself, and the activities and initiatives on and around the vast 120 square miles of this 'Wet Sahara.'

It is a dynamic story in a dynamic bay, and though Cedric might seem to be the original 'Joe Cool,' he has observed some dramatic developments. From plans to build a bridge and a barrage across the Bay, to attempts to send up rockets towards that other 'infinity' called space. Yet Cedric has always had his feet on the ground, or at least on the sands, ever since he started out as a 'fisherman on foot' more than 70 years ago. That is why his siren warnings about the effects of climate change in the Bay have to be taken seriously.

This is not a biography of his life, from his background in the fishing community of Flookburgh on the Cartmel Peninsula, to the post of Queen's Guide. That story has been told well in a series of excellent books, though you will pick up most of the salient points on the way through. This book takes Cedric's story forward, looking at the health and well-being of the Bay and some of the issues affecting its surrounding towns and communities.

It includes Cedric's take on what has happened, and what is happening – from the mainstream, to the quirky, to the off-beat, and the downright funny aspects of life. It is a kind of 'Baywatch' with a difference, though without Pamela Anderson or David Hasselhoff centre stage. It is not definitive or all-inclusive, but it is an overview of the ebbs and flows of life in and around the Bay. It is fascinating, and often amusing, to hear the measured views of a keen-eyed observer, who has seen much happen in the 'Wet Sahara' to which he has been 'wedded' for the past 70-odd years.

His real marriage has been to "my beautiful Olive." Few people know that in his late twenties, Cedric took on the responsibility of looking after Olive's four children, following the untimely death of her husband. Then, a few years after Cedric and Olive's wedding, along came their daughter Jean. Looking after five children is quite an awesome task for anyone, especially when you realise that the eldest was only 14 years younger than Ced himself. However, they all rubbed along together in Guide's Farm, the rudimentary, grace-and-favour homestead that for many years had no electricity, still has no central heating, that once flooded, and that is hardly a palace by the sea. But it has been 'home' for 55 years, and Cedric and Olive have been happy with their often hand-to-mouth, make-do-and-mend lifestyle.

They are both dear friends of mine, and it has been a pleasure to write this labour-of-love book; to get to know Cedric and Olive even better; to reflect the qualities and the contributions of Cedric's helpers on his cross-bay walks; and to get to grips with life on the Bay. Cedric likes the result: I hope you do too.

Legend of Morecambe Bay

IT was always going to be a tough task – and a delicate manoeuvre.

When and how was 86-year-old Cedric Robinson going to hand on his duties as the Queen's Guide to the Morecambe Bay Sands?

And who was going to pick up the baton, knowing it would be in the limelight of the most celebrated, respected and much-loved holder of the prestigious post? Cedric's reputation, his feats of endurance, his application and his fundraising activities inevitably cast a long shadow.

To many, Cedric is a legend in his own lifetime. The last of a dying breed who see self-sacrifice, kindness and unsung service as a way of life.

He's certainly got character, and is a character, in the best sense of that term. Following in his footsteps is no easy task for anyone. After all, Cedric has been the Queen's custodian of the sands for 55 years – the longest-ever guide, serving the longest-ever reigning monarch.

He has turned what was becoming an archaic piece of history into a useful, modern-day recreational activity, taking up to 10,000 people a year across the Bay on sponsored walks for charity. It's reckoned that up to 500,000 fundraising walkers have been guided across the sands from Arnside to Kents Bank under Cedric's leadership. In doing so, it's reckoned by some that Cedric has walked the equivalent of twice round the world, and helped raise thousands upon thousands of pounds for those in need of help and assistance.

THRESHOLD OF HAPPINESS: A younger Cedric and wife Olive on the doorstep of their home, Guide's Farm, near Grange-over-Sands. (Picture by Peter Thompson)

How can a man of such humble origins become a person known and revered by millions across the country, even across the world? How can this man of simple but sound values have given such great pleasure to so many? He has introduced thousands to the magnificence of this stretch of North West coastal Britain, hitherto unknown to the vast majority of people . . . and all this for a 'salary' of £15 a year.

Handing on the baton – in his case, a stout walking staff – is a manoeuvre that aims to achieve three things – maintaining Cedric's dignity after his long years of sacrifice and service; obtaining security for him and his Olive, now in her mid-nineties – "I obviously like the older woman"; and setting a transitional course of action that offers continuity and safety to the task in hand.

Cedric has been out in the Bay as a fisherman, shrimper and cockler since he was 14. In time-honoured fashion, his forays into the Bay were by foot, horse and cart, and ultimately by tractor on the vast expanses of tide-swept sand, criss-crossed by the ever-changing river channels. Boats were unnecessary, even a hindrance for Bay fishermen, who put their nets on staves in the channels, collecting their catch when the tide flows in and then ebbs out again.

Back then, in his younger days, he could not have realised that he would become the Queen's longest-serving Guide to the Sands. Nor would Her Majesty have realised that she too would ultimately break Queen Victoria's record reign to become the longest-serving monarch herself. A proud achievement for both of them.

Cedric has met the Queen, formally at Buckingham Palace when she conferred an MBE on her Guide to the Sands, and at functions and dinners in Cumbria and Lancashire, which he has attended quietly and without fuss.

He has one big regret, in that he always wished he could have escorted Her Majesty across the sands, but it never happened.

Cedric adds: "I took Prince Philip across on a horse and buggy, and you never know, it would be nice to accompany Prince Charles across one of these days, or one of the younger princes. I'm sure they would like that. Prince Charles is very much aware of, and appreciative of, the natural world, and he understands the threats from climate change. I think he would relish the opportunity."

As the years rolled on, 'Ced' always wanted to chalk up 50 years' service to the Queen – and to the thousands of sponsored walkers, who have raised millions of pounds for charity over the years. That having been achieved back in 2013, he set himself a new challenge – "to keep buggering on," as Winston Churchill put it so eloquently, in his own inimitable fashion.

Now, as Cedric passes 55 years in the post, he has decided to go into 'a transitional period,' offering a 'guiding hand' and assistance to his successor, passing on the ways and wonders of guided walks across Morecambe Bay.

The overall task is quite simple – to ensure that as much as possible is done to find a route for the safe passage of up to 500 walkers on each of the season's 20 or so eight-mile treks across the shifting, and potentially-treacherous, sands of the Bay. However, there is much more to it than that. Judgement, timing, decision-making, people skills and ease of manner all come to it. Cedric's quiet authority and his firm but no-fuss leadership skills will be a hard act to follow. But with grace and goodwill, these values and characteristics can be passed on.

The new guide, Michael Wilson – from Flookburgh – has Cedric's blessing. Like Cedric, Michael comes from a long line of Morecambe Bay fishermen and cocklers, and he comes to the post of Guide in his forties, ten years older than Cedric in his early days.

Being the Queen's Guide means that an allowance of £15 a year is paid to Cedric, though this is after deduction of 'rent' for Guide's Farm, a pretty rudimentary grace and favour dwelling that has been the home of the Queen's Guide for time immemorial. The first guide was appointed back in the 1530s, during the reign of Henry VIII.

Michael has his own home within the Flookburgh fishing community, where Cedric also grew up, then carried on the family fishing tradition, in exactly the same way that Michael has done years later. As such, Michael is more than happy for Cedric and Olive to stay put in Guide's Farm, while he stays on in Flookburgh with his family and friends. To everyone's relief and satisfaction, this means that the Guide Over Sands Trust – the body responsible for the walks and the guide appointments – have been able to allow Ced and Olive to remain in what has been their home for more than half a century.

Cedric has never been hung up with what some people call 'the finer things in life.' Material possessions and the so-called 'high life' are not in his vision, his views, or his vocabulary. He has never been on a plane, and has never had an official annual holiday, let alone holiday pay. He has hardly ever left the Bay, and has lived a meagre but fulfilling life, living out of the Bay. His 'riches' are in what he does, in meeting and helping people, in chatting with folk and making conversation – and, of course, in being out there walking the sands.

It is no secret to Cedric's friends that he and Olive – a stalwart who has been at her husband's right hand throughout his tenure as Guide – were worried about what would happen to them when he finally gave up planting his footsteps in the sand as official guide.

Now, it can be revealed, a carefully-choreographed manoeuvre was worked out that gives Cedric security of tenure, while he oversees the handover to the new post holder, acting as an advisor and ambassador. He will join Michael in doing the vital recce before each walk, while also accompanying him on the walks. This will allow Michael to bed in to the position, while giving walkers both continuity and peace of mind, in the knowledge that Cedric is still on board to help out. He will be there, alongside Michael, to welcome old friends and newcomers alike. As ever, Olive and

ONE FOR THE ALBUM: Some of the Robinson clan (left to right) – Cedric's stepson Paul Nickson; Cedric, Olive and their daughter Jean; Olive's mother Olive Healey; Cedric's father Bill; with a friend of Jean standing behind them all.

daughter Jean, will be at the end of each walk to welcome people across the finishing line – before they cross the railway line to Kents Bank Station.

Cedric is only too aware that the Bay itself is a dynamic and ever-changing place in every respect, and he admits: "Nothing is forever. I know that, from living on the sands all my life. I think it's time to begin the process of ensuring the future of the walks.

It's time to begin the process of handing over the reigns and the responsibilities.

"I have every confidence in Michael learning the ropes. He is from a good fishing family, like me, and knows the Bay and its ways as good as anyone. But I will say one thing: a fisherman can take a risk, a guide cannot. That is the key thing that I have learned and it is the key message to everyone concerned. It may be unpopular to cancel a walk if there are too many dangers and no safe route, but it has to be done – and out there, you can't cut corners. The guide has the safety of hundreds of people in his hands."

Living with the vagaries of the sands, and the evolution of the Bay, is a way of life, and Cedric can now pass on his considerable know-how and nous, his wit and his wisdom, to his named successor over the forthcoming seasons.

Of course, some things seem timeless, and the Bay needs no 'sell' to the public at large. It has a deep effect on all who visit its shores, including leading travel writer Bill Bryson, who says: "Morecambe Bay may be the most beautiful in Britain." Broadcaster and author Gyles Brandreth is a huge fan too, describing the sunset in the Bay as being "as good as you might get in the Aegean," adding: "Forget Corfu, get up to Morecambe."

However, being so close to nature, Cedric knows only too well that 'change' is constant and inevitable. But are things in the Bay changing faster than normal? What of climate change and global warming?

With more than eight decades of experience and keen-eyed observation, Ced has his views – and a warning for future generations.

I can scarcely believe that Derian House has been taking part in cross-bay walks with Cedric for 22 years!

I had absolutely no idea what to expect when I first drove up to Grange-over-Sands and Guide's Farm to meet Cedric and his delightful wife Olive, to discuss the possibility of the hospice taking part in one of his famous walks. What I found, was a delightfully unassuming, quietly spoken man, with a calm air of assurance, and a great sense of humour, who knows the Kent Sands like his own back yard, which essentially, of course, is exactly what it is!

That afternoon, sitting in Cedric's garden in the sunshine, listening to his wonderful stories about the Bay, and supplied with tea and cakes by Olive, his lovely wife, who was the main point of contact for charities wanting to sign up for a walk, was one of the most entertaining and fascinating I have ever spent, and it was with great reluctance that I finally took my leave of them.

It was the shape of things to come, and year on year since then, Derian House has staged its annual Morecambe Bay Walk which has proved so popular with its supporters. It's an event which sees them trekking across the sand, negotiating the channels, and just occasionally experiencing the thrill of "real quicksand", all on a mission to raise as much money as possible for the hospice, with Cedric, staff in hand, leading us forward like some latter day Moses!

Since that first walk in 1997, more than £150,000 has been raised for the hospice, none of which would have been possible without Cedric's generosity and expertise.

So, on behalf of myself, and everyone at Derian House Children's Hospice, I would like to say an immense 'thank you' to Cedric. Without doubt, we, and many other charities would have been much the poorer, both financially and experientially without him!

Susie Poppitt, Fundraising Consultant,
Derian House Children's Hospice, Chorley.

Cedric, climate change, and the Bay

IT doesn't take official scientific reports to convince Cedric about the effects of global warming and climate change.

The man who has spent more than 70 years on the sands points towards the window of his Bay-front cottage and says: "The evidence is there, right outside my front door."

He adds: "A couple of summers ago, it was the worst I've known for wind and rain together. That was the key – together. I used to rarely have to cancel a walk over my 55 years as Guide, but I had to postpone four weekends that year, then another lot the following year.

"I've never seen water like it in the main river channel, and I've been out there on the sands since I was 14 years old after I left school to work with my father out on the sands. My old dad lived to the grand old age of 102, and he had 90 years' experience as a fisherman, cockler and shrimper out there in the Bay. I remember him telling me: 'It never blows hard on a high tide – but it does now, lad.'

"He told me: 'Things are changing. You get the same signs for wet weather as you do for fine weather. The old saying: 'Red skies at night, shepherd's delight,' and, 'Red skies in the morning, shepherd's warning,' doesn't necessarily hold true any more.' It used to do as a rock-solid law. I know that. I'm an old hand at looking for weather signs to best guide my activities out there in the Bay. Red sky is still a useful indicator but there are variations now."

WHAT A BORE! A Morecambe Bay tidal bore roars up the shallows at speeds of up to 9 knots, moving tons of material in a matter of moments. (Pictures by Paul Nickson)

If the observations of Cedric and his father, Bill, are correct, the significance could be great. The 'red sky' weather indicator has stood virtually unquestioned for two millennia, ever since it was first written down in the Gospel of St Matthew in the Bible. The red sky at night, caused by the setting sun's rays shining through dust and small particles trapped in the atmosphere by high pressure, has traditionally indicated fine weather. In the morning, the same visual phenomenon forewarns 'foul weather . . . for the sky is red and lowering.'

Cedric is the first to remind you that he is no trained scientist, but he obviously believes that climate changes have made the old weather axioms questionable, to say the least. Certainly, he thinks that the observations by him and his father over the last hundred years or so are a useful starting point for thought and discussion about what is happening to the weather and its effects on Mother Nature and the Bay.

Cedric is deadly serious about weather changes: after all's said and done, it does inform him for taking walkers safely across the Bay, and for "living out of the Bay as much as possible." But he can't help making you laugh, with his droll sense of humour, as he adds: "Of course, they say round here that if there's any red sky on the horizon, it means that Sellafield has gone up. Or it could be Heysham Atomic Power Station if it's red skies over Morecambe way."

Back on the serious side, Cedric points out the evidence he has for believing that something – "probably global warming and climate change" – has to be responsible for the changes he's observed over the time span of three or four generations. He is adamant when he says: "I can certainly see changes – the tides are rising, they're definitely coming in higher. The Bay was much more stable in my younger days, though it has always been a shifting environment physically. That has to be acknowledged – but that's nature in all its wonderment.

"When I was appointed, back in 1963, we had good summers. I'm not an old man just being nostalgic, with distorted memories of good times gone by, though I do have happy thoughts about the days of my youth and as a younger man. No, I can say, hand on heart, that the crossings in the Bay were much shallower back then, and that change must be down to the effects of the rains swelling the rivers, and, of course, the volume of the tides coming in. We've always had thunderstorms, yes, but not the endless, torrential downpours we have experienced in more recent times. It's a case of more rain and more wind, and they come together at the same time, more often than not."

He adds: "When I'm out there testing the sands and finding a safe route for walkers, more and more I see white horses – or strong wave action, as some people call it – in the channels. And that can make it six inches deeper. On my way to a walk, I often stop at Levens Bridge to look down at the state of the River Kent, which drains much of what is now South Cumbria, and goes on to be our main crossing on the Bay Walks. I look at the level and speed of the river and I can judge how that will affect the walks.

"Then there are the tides – and remember, no tide is ever the same. You can make assumptions, but you have to always be prepared to be surprised. All this has an effect on the Bay, and definitely, change is afoot."

Scientists across the Bay at Lancaster University can verify Cedric's observations: the blunt fact is that there has been a 30 per cent seasonal increase in rainfall in the Morecambe Bay area over the past 50 years.

The staggering increase, concentrated over the autumn and winter months of October to January, triggered the devastating Lake District flooding that swept through Keswick, Cockermouth and Kendal in 2009, followed by Storm Desmond in 2015. The rivers flowing into Morecambe Bay and in the channels through the Bay, have seen a corresponding increase, reinforcing the observations of Cedric from a layman's perspective.

The scientific findings are given credence by the fact that rainfall monitoring for the area has been carried out each and every day over the past 50 years, ever since Lancaster University opened its weather centre back in 1967, on the hills at Hazelrigg, just across the M6 motorway from Lancaster University.

Dr James Heath, of Lancaster University's Environment Centre, and the person who does the daily readings at Hazelrigg, says the evidence clearly points to global warming and climate change as the motors for this phenomenon. He sees the bigger world picture and the local scene only too well – and his findings corroborate Cedric's observations over the last 70 years or so. Dr Heath says the figures locally show that something is changing, and affecting the weather of the Bay, quite dramatically.

He points to the devastating Lake District floods of 2009 – with Cockermouth most affected – and the 2015 blitz of Storm Desmond, both of which occurred in that pre-Christmas winter period. Dr Heath, who has a Durham University degree in Biology, before he undertook his PhD on the effects of rising carbon dioxide concentrations on tree and forest water use, points to the more recent rainfall figures he has recorded. Not to put too fine a point on it, they are astounding.

Hazelrigg, just east of Morecambe Bay, received 556.2mm of rainfall in November and December, 2015 – "a significant leap from the average of 227.4mm over the same period." Sitting at his work desk at Hazelrigg, and studying his charts, Dr Heath adds: "That's a 245 per cent increase in rainfall, and the flooding of the Cumbrian and Lancashire areas followed, as sure as night follows day."

On the bigger picture, Dr Heath says the Storm Desmond cause was in part attributed to the "El Niño effect, where unusually high sea surface temperatures in the Eastern Pacific affected the weather around the world." He adds: "Here in the UK we saw an increase in stormy weather conditions from the Atlantic, leading to a greater likelihood of extreme weather events." More specifically, during

CHECKING OUT THE WEATHER: Lancaster University scientist, Dr James Heath, at work measuring rainfall and weather conditions in and around Morecambe Bay at his desk in Hazelrigg Weather Station, on the hills above Lancaster.

Storm Desmond, a huge volume of moist air from the Caribbean swept over the British Isles, causing 'unusually heavy rainfall and strong winds.'

Sea temperatures over the north Atlantic were several degrees above average at the time, and Dr Heath says: "Global warming will worsen this process. For every increase of one degree Celsius, the atmosphere can hold 6 per cent more moisture, and that means abnormally heavy rainfall. Locally, it's not raining more often, but each rainfall event is more intense because of the increased temperatures."

In the Lake District and north Pennine areas that fringe Morecambe Bay, that warming can lead to a triple-whammy, effect. Firstly, there is more energy in the atmosphere to drive the

SIMPLY RED: Morecambe Bay has always been famous for its amazing red sunsets . . . but do they still bring delight to shepherds?

frontal and low pressure systems that give us rainfall in the North West. Secondly, the warmer air can hold more water, and as this rises over the hills in our area, it dumps more of it. Thirdly, as the atmosphere releases rain, it also releases more heat, rather like a household fridge warms at the back through condensation of the liquid inside. That heat drives further convection and more rain ensues. And there is no doubt that a large part of the initial increase in temperature is man-made.

Dr Heath explains: "The initial Industrial Revolution sparked it, but changes have got much more rapid since the 1980s, with an acceleration in temperature increases. There was a slow down in the middle of the 20th Century, possibly due to natural causes as well as increases in particulate pollution. But then it picked up, tying in with an accelerating rate of increase in atmospheric carbon dioxide concentrations. This is due to a continued increase in the use of fossil fuels by western countries, as well as the rapidly industrialising countries, such as India and China."

And what of the recent intensity of the dry summer of 2018? Dr Heath points to a recent study by the Met Office which suggests that human-induced climate change has made the 2018 record-breaking summer heatwave about 30 times more likely than it would be naturally. We may all have enjoyed the good weather, but the warning signs are there too.

Cedric may not have the scientific training, though his reputation and contribution have earned him no less than 20 awards and honours, including an Honorary Doctorate from the Science and Technology Faculty at Lancaster University, which has maintained its position in the *Guardian*'s University 'Top Ten' League Table.

As a respected 'Man of the Sands,' Cedric's feedback makes convincing, even potentially alarming, reading. Nostalgia is certainly not the driving force when he recalls his father and fellow fishermen standing on sand bars at the edge of the deep channels, with long, pronged forks in hand, waiting to spear passing salmon. He also recalls watching shoals of porpoise swimming by, "another sure sign that salmon were there for the taking." Nowadays, neither salmon nor porpoise can be readily observed in the Bay. As Cedric confirms: "I haven't seen one salmon all last season, and that tells me that something has changed."

Nor does he often hear the plaintive call of the curlew, that long-billed bird of the surrounding upper moorlands of Cumbria, Lancashire and Yorkshire that has traditionally come down from the hills in autumn and winter, seeking food and warmer climes in the Bay area. On the positive side, the gulls are still there in profusion, and the beautiful and haunting sound of the oystercatcher can be heard by walkers as they trek across the vast expanses of sand.

With all the concerns about plastics in the oceans, what are Cedric's observations about this hot topic? He says: "You do see torn plastic bags and plastic bottle debris on the shoreline quite often, and that is not a good thing. I don't see them out on the sands and in the water of the Bay so much, which is, hopefully, a good sign. But maybe I'm being naive. We're told that the plastic threat to sea life is in small particle form. You can't see the particles, and if they are there, it's going to be harmful in some way. Whatever the case, plastic debris in the sea is not good for anyone or anything."

But there are positives and heartening developments, and human interventions that can help reverse the problems that blight our world. Naturally, Cedric is keen on habitat and education initiatives around the Bay – and that is addressed in later chapters.

Ruskin the environmentalist

IRONICALLY, the man often credited with first mooting the idea of man-made climate change settled just 20 miles from Cedric's beloved bay back in the late 19th Century.

John Ruskin is renowned for being an artist, aesthete, humanitarian

THE SEA SHALL HAVE THEM: The salt marshes on the Grange-over-Sands side of the Bay are being eroded as the River Kent's channel swings back towards the shoreline. (Picture by Paul Nickson)

and radical campaigner for social justice, and measures to eliminate poverty for the working class in Britain during the Industrial Revolution. However, it is little realised that this man of many parts is credited by many to be a founding father of environmentalism.

Ruskin, a university academic in Oxford, first articulated the phrase "the plague wind," a term he used to describe the industrial pollution he encountered in London. In later life, he moved to South Lakeland, to live in Brantwood, a wonderfully-positioned residence overlooking Coniston Water, just a short distance north of Morecambe Bay. Today, his home of nearly 30 years is dedicated to him as a historic house, museum and centre for the arts.

However, Brantwood Director, Howard Hull, stresses how Ruskin constantly thought about the "connection and consequences" of everything, with all things being interrelated. "So, although his thoughts on climate may surprise some people, Ruskin's view on climate change and nature is linked up and connected," says Mr Hull, who has been Director at Ruskin's Lakeland home for nearly 23 years now, and who is also the long-standing Director of the Ruskin Foundation.

Mr Hull explains: "Ruskin saw nature as the centre of understanding life, and also the basis for social justice. He saw 'laws for life' in nature, which he thought encouraged cooperation. In contrast, Charles Darwin viewed nature as fomenting competition, which Ruskin referred to as 'the laws of death.'"

Mr Hull added: "He went much further than people around him to predict that pollution was destroying things. Many people could see that, for example, volcanic activity had an effect on the atmosphere, but Ruskin saw it was not just natural phenomenon that were causing changes. He saw that a lot of change was caused by the industrial processes that were taking off at the time. Then he widened the proposition, right down to the way we treated each other. He said that living in cramped and insanitary cities created by the Industrial Revolution meant human beings were being degraded too, just like the climate.

"He had a concept called 'ilth' – that's ILTH or 'ill health' as opposed to 'health,' and he thought the environment could suffer 'ill health' because of bad treatment. He thought that any one action we do had immediate and lasting impacts on us, many of which we cannot even see."

It's a lot to get your mind across, and even though Ruskin was expansive, philosophical and imaginative with his thoughts, he was quite obscure with his concepts and had a florid and eccentric style of writing.

However, his use of the term 'grey clouds of the plague wind' is seen as having deep significance in identifying how man was changing the natural order with his industrial activity. In 1871, Ruskin made his famous 'Stormclouds' speech that identified a 'dry, black veil, through which no ray of sunshine could penetrate.' He said: "It looks partly as if it were made of poisonous smoke," adding that where he was in London, "there are at least 200 furnace chimneys in a two-square mile area around me."

Ruskin said: "Never before, in a lifetime of monitoring nature's movements, have I seen such springs and summers." Just 150 years on, Cedric Robinson and his father observed things happening that they had never experienced before, particularly involving rain and wind conditions.

Thirty two years before his landmark 'Stormclouds' speech, Ruskin had supported the Meteorological Society, calling for 'methodical and simultaneous observations' to be made throughout the world. Yet, despite his scientific rigour, Ruskin had a spiritual, almost mystical side, which made him feel that the 'plague wind' might partly be due to the shifting to and fro of 'dead men's souls.' This concept may seem at odds with his intellectual approach and his rigour. Nevertheless, he is credited with creating an environmental awareness on the bigger canvas of life.

Obviously, he could not have foreseen the scale of the climate change phenomenon of today, with China and India joining America as major polluting nations. However, his views were prophetic in highlighting the need to remedy the stresses and strains of man's relationship with nature. No doubt he would have wholeheartedly approved of the Paris Climate Change Conference of 2015, where nearly 200 countries pledged to decrease their greenhouse gas carbon emissions. Surely, he would have endorsed the aim to halt the rise of global temperatures, keeping them from rising 1.5 degrees Celsius above pre-industrial levels.

* The pace of change has been exponential, and maybe it gives historical perspective to realise that four years after Ruskin died in 1900, Cedric's father Bill was born in a fisherman's cottage in the little village of Flookburgh, just a short hop from Ruskin's beloved retreat of Brantwood.

As a brand new fundraiser way back in 2008 and less than two weeks into the job, I was asked to attend the Morecambe Bay Walk, 'Just so you can see how we do these

things,' said the Fundraising Manager, as he cheerily waved me goodbye, mouthing, 'See you on the other side in about three hours.'

I nervously wondered what on earth had possessed me to apply for a job that left me alone to do an 8-mile hike across the sands, with forty people clamouring for t-shirts, and no clue what I was supposed to do next. I needn't have worried, because Cedric had it all under control and as he picked his way across the treacherous sands, guiding several hundred people safely to the other side, I marvelled at him.

I still marvel at him to this day because, in 2008, Cedric was already well into his 70s and had been traversing the shifting sands several times a month since he became the Queen's Guide in 1963. It's not just about the crossings though; I am well aware of how much work and planning has to go into every walk because the sands change every day. I am a fundraiser after all. It's what we do, and it's what Cedric has done magnificently for over 55 years.

If I think about how much money has been raised by all the charities crossing the sands under his expert guidance across all those decades, it must run into untold millions and all because of Cedric. He is a truly remarkable man!

**Michelle King, Corporate & Trusts Fundraiser,
Bury Hospice.**

Following in Cedric's footsteps

MICHAEL Wilson has broad shoulders . . . and size 10 feet. It's just as well, since he's got big boots to fill, following in Cedric Robinson's footsteps.

Just like Cedric, Michael comes from a long-established Flookburgh fishing family. At the age of 46, he's 16 years older than Cedric was when he took on the role of Guide to the Sands. Even so, Michael has a long time ahead of him to fulfil his remit of taking walkers safely across the vast expanse of Morecambe Bay.

He lives and works out of his home and tackle yard in Flookburgh's Main Street, opposite the house where Cedric's dad, Bill, used to live. So Michael knows the family well, and readily admits: "Following Cedric is quite an honour. I'm perfectly aware that his are big, big footsteps in which to follow."

Continuing the theme, he adds: "When I was sounded out by the Trust, I told them: 'I don't want to step on Cedric's toes in any way.' But they told me: 'Don't worry about that. Cedric has recommended you.' That was a great feeling, and so I agreed to it, with Cedric's blessing. It's quite an honour to be recommended by him and then to be wanted by the Trust.

"Of course, I'll be different to a degree. Everyone has their own personality and style, but I would like to think I'm a personable type, like Cedric. In truth, Cedric is a bit of a showman – that's part of his charm. He's not a show-off type, but he obviously likes

GETTING IN GEAR: Cedric's chosen
successor, Michael Wilson, on his tractor
outside his fisherman's cottage in Flookburgh.

the attention and a bit of the limelight when he's out there with a crowd. He's a bit like a god to a lot of his following. I'm sure that he likes being on TV and in the newspapers – and he deserves that recognition and that status after all those years of helping to raise thousands and thousands of pounds. He'll be a hard act to follow but you can only do your best and get on with it."

Michael, who has been out fishing since he was a lad himself, admits: "Like anyone in a fishing family, I know the Bay. I've been going out with my dad, and often with my son Jake nowadays, for all of my life. You get to know the ways of it all and the lay of the land, or should that be sand, though you always have the greatest respect for the changes that are possible – the sands, the rivers, and the tides above all.

"But I'm glad Cedric is staying on board and will come out with me to test the conditions, mark out a route for the walkers, and then be on the walks themselves. There's no conflict at all. Someone has to follow Cedric and he knows that. He's all right with that. I think that in his heart, he's looking forward to the new arrangements. I popped round to look at the tide tables with him, and allocate the walk times accordingly. He'd written them down in principle and he was very warm and welcoming. This transitional arrangement is best for both of us. He keeps his dignity and involvement and I get his help and experience. It seems a good arrangement to me."

He added: "I'm amazed at Cedric's stamina and willpower, even now in his eighties. Even so, he had an accident when his horse and cart nipped him, and his hernia operation took its toll. I think he's actually looking forward to the new arrangements. It takes the strain off him, though I think he'll be out there on the sands for the rest of his life. I understand that, only too well. It's a way of life for us both. That's what his family and mine were brought up to do."

One thing Michael is glad about is that Cedric will have security of tenure in Guide Farm, where he lives with, and looks after, his wife Olive. For 55 years, she has acted as his invaluable, unpaid 'secretary,' taking all the phone calls and keeping walkers and charities informed of weather conditions and the situation out there on the sands.

Now that Olive is in her nineties, she is no longer able to do this. So, the task of organising the walks will fall to the Trust, who will pay Michael a salary to do the walks, in lieu of the rent-free tenure that Cedric has had in Guide's Farm.

Michael reveals: "I'm happy to stay in my own house in Flookburgh, where I have my yard with all my fishing gear; where my family live, including my mother and father; and very importantly, where my son Jake goes to school. I'll carry on fishing from here, and let Cedric get on with his life in Kents Bank. I'm glad he has security of tenure there. He's a bit of a carer for Olive now, and he needs that security."

Like Cedric, Michael intends to continue with the Arnside to Kents Bank route across the Bay, rather than vary it. He says: "It seems to be ideal for everyone. Walkers can travel easily and readily to Arnside by train or by car, then have a bite to eat there, meet-up and register with their charities before walking the eight-miles or so across the Bay with me, Cedric, and the helpers. At Kents Bank, they end up at the railway station, and can either be picked up there or catch a train for the four or five-minute journey back to Arnside across the Kent Estuary Viaduct, which is a very scenic route in itself. Fish and chips, or whatever, and then back home. A perfect day. Cedric worked it all out, and I'm happy to follow suit."

Bearing in mind the changes taking place in the Bay, and the increasing volatility of the Kent Channel, with the fluctuating quicksand areas, some walks have had to be postponed over recent years. However, Michael thinks he has the solution, and says: "In these circumstances, rather than postpone the weekend's walks, I think it best to offer a walk out to the Kent Channel, maybe across it and back under supervision if it's safe, and then back to the Arnside shore. I think that will be more acceptable to the charities, who can still call it their Morecambe Bay fundraiser, and collect their valuable sponsorship donations. It's do-able and if the charities agree, that could be the ideal answer, instead of the huge disappointment of cancelling the event, with all the loss of vital revenue for the charities. I know how important this event is to their members and supporters. For many charities, it's their main fundraiser of the year. With a bit of sideways thinking, it can be still, whatever the conditions out there in the Bay. Providing there is an established safe route, everyone will benefit."

Like most people, Michael is amazed at the scale of the operation that Cedric has built up over his 55 years of activity on the sands. He says: "Almost single-handedly, Cedric has created a huge 'fundraising machine,' for want of a better expression. Thousands of pounds have been raised for good causes, thousands of people have been helped, and the walks have given massive enjoyment, and a sense of achievement to so many."

He says: "Tourism and leisure has become a huge industry, and is important to this area of South Lakeland and the coast. People have more time and are able to do more with their time. They used to have to work six days a week, but with the shorter working week, early retirement and holidays, people have more time and are prepared to do something active and useful. I've noticed that a lot of older people have put their time and effort into helping charities. Many of them seem to help organise the walk for their particular charity, and then take part in it themselves. They want to help, and I want to help them, just like Cedric has over all those years."

But again like Cedric, Michael is a fisherman first and foremost, though he's looking forward to his new challenge. He has to admit: "I'll never pass Cedric's years of service and I don't think anyone will. I think his 55-year record will stand forever. At the age of 46, you would hope I would have 20 years or so in front of me, taking up the baton, but Cedric can rest easy about his achievement."

Michael's family involvement as Morecambe Bay fishing folk

goes back to his great, great, great grandfather, and he says: "My dad John is now in his seventies, but he keeps up his interest, and he keeps a diary too. He may have a reputation as a man of few words, but he knows about the Bay. He can remember catching hundreds of salmon back in the 1960s. There must have been thousands going up the Kent channel back then, but not now. There are no salmon here, and in the Ribble Estuary only a few were caught last year. I think it's a result of over-fishing, disease and pollution, yet the environment people didn't seem to realise what was going on until it was too late. They've only taken the salmon licence off us fairly recently, and that was too late in itself."

Like Cedric, Michael has observed the ebbs and flows of fishing fortune over the years. He says: "There are a few sea trout, tons of plaice and flooks, but the quality of shrimps has decreased, with dire catches in recent times. However, there are cockles all over the Bay. If there's a lot of fresh water, they can be killed off, but the recent hot, dry summer meant an abundance of them. People talk about over-fishing but nature is the biggest factor in my opinion. We're at the mercy of nature because it's such a vast, open bay."

Michael has no doubt that cockling will survive Brexit and any new rules and regulations "because the demand is there." He points out that most of the produce goes to Spain, France and Holland, much of the harvest travelling in what is known as the 'Cockle Wagon.' Catches in the North West are taken to a collecting point in Liverpool, then travel in tanks aboard the 40-ton articulated 'Cockle Wagon,' arriving purified through the swishing movement en route, arriving ready to eat in Rotterdam.

Like Cedric, Michael has learned to take everything in his stride – like the day when he was asked to help launch a space rocket out in the Bay! Michael says: "Nothing takes you by surprise in this job. I received a telephone call one day asking me to help with a mission to send people up to the edge of outer space in a rocket. "They call it 'space tourism' today, but back then, in the late 90s, it was into the unknown. A private company from Manchester wanted to trial their unmanned rocket over the Bay and asked me to tow it out with my tractor to the launch site at Cartmel Wharf, which is a sandbank about three miles out. I didn't know what to expect, but it worked, and they did it on two more occasions. Once, it came down in the sea and we had to wait until the tide went out again to retrieve it. It helps to make life interesting, doesn't it?"

On the cross-bay walking front, Michael says he intends to go round from Flookburgh to Arnside by train to meet and address the walkers before leading them out with his helpers. He will welcome the guys who helped Cedric and has three pals who have expressed an interest in helping out. With a wry smile, he says: "Many of the assistants are retired people who want to help and get involved. It's going to be a bit like *Last of the Summer Wine*!"

Joking apart, he stresses that safety is paramount on walks. He says: "It's very different from going out fishing. As a fisherman, you take calculated risks to make your catch. You go right down to the last ten minutes before the tide turns to make that all-important last sack. But when you are leading walkers, that cannot be the case at all. You never take that risk – but there again, you never have to."

One of our aims at St Catherine's Hospice in Lancashire is to inspire people into action to support our good work, ensuring the experience is fun and rewarding for all those involved. Cedric Robinson and his  Morecambe Bay Walk have helped us achieve this many times over, with hundreds of people from all walks of life. It's only thanks to Cedric's detailed knowledge of this beautiful – yet potentially dangerous – stretch of coastline, that charities both large and small, have been able to harness their fundraising potential, offering supporters a unique opportunity to conquer a challenge which is off limits to them alone.

We have been lucky enough to be part of his cross-bay walks for many years. Cedric has safely led our wonderful supporters along the iconic route, helping them to achieve something amazing and enabling them to raise thousands of pounds in sponsorship for St Catherine's in the process.

As a local charity we depend on the generosity and efforts of supporters to raise £3.7m of our annual £5.4m running costs – the revenue raised through the Morecambe Bay Walk over the years has made an important contribution to this. Every income stream is vital, as we work to help people affected by conditions like cancer, motor neurone disease and heart failure to have a good quality of life, right to the end of life.

On behalf of everyone at St Catherine's and all the patients and families we care for, we'd like to say a huge thank you to Cedric for his incredible contribution.

Lorraine Charlesworth,
Director of Community and Income,
St Catherine's Hospice, Preston.

Senses and sensibilities,
a personal pleasure

THERE'S nothing quite like it. Walking across Morecambe Bay is an awakening of all five of the senses – sight, sound, smell, touch and taste.

It's a heady cocktail, a connection with nature itself, and your feelings. Yet it's much more than that. It's highly personal and completely communal at the same time. You alone experience the unfolding delights and sensations during the eight-mile trek, but much of the joy is the pleasure of doing it alongside scores – if not hundreds – of others. It's a feeling of collective camaraderie, of common cause, of mutual satisfaction. It's what former football manager Arsene Wenger called 'togetherness.' Forget your tribal differences, he understood only too well the power and dynamics of the group.

But what is the cross-bay experience actually like? Just what does it offer and engender, being out there in the middle of 120 square miles of vastness?

One thing is for sure: it always feels good. Doing the walk, for the first time, or the 21st time, is an experience that does you good, and makes you feel good about others. It's a challenge that leads to a sense of achievement. It's healthy, low cost, and accessible to the many. You do see a few people who fit into the category of: 'All the gear, no idea,' but no-one makes an issue of it. Some walkers have the latest, super-branded, washable trainers, and that's fine. Others do it barefoot, though the initial ridge sections can be tough on unhardened feet.

But the sheer joy of being out there – all ages, all backgrounds – is overwhelmingly pleasurable. It's something different, a 'bucket list' experience that many people want to do for just one time in their lifetime. Then they find themselves going back, for another annual feel-good experience. In a busy and complex world – with all its demands, stresses and strains – it's an exhilarating experience that is hard to beat. A manageable achievement too, more often than not with the bonus of raising funds for a cause dear to your heart. For many, it doesn't get much better.

The sense of SIGHT is given a major boost as you walk off from the shore at White Creek, after trekking from Arnside to the edge of the Kent Estuary. Out there in front of you is the stunning vista of the 'Wet Sahara' of 120 square miles of sand and water. As Cedric often says: "The scenery changes a hundred times a day," with the golden hues of sandbanks; the glistening silvery water; the 'big skies' above; and the distant shapes of the surrounding fells, hills and mountains. To the east are the hills and moorland fells of Lancashire and Yorkshire, with the distinctive shape of Ingleborough on the horizon. Beyond the northern shore are the Lakeland fells and mountains, while out west are the vague outlines of buildings in Barrow, with wind turbines off shore. If you're a back marker for Cedric, the sight of up to 500 walkers snaking out in front of you across the estuary is unforgettable. All with a common purpose and a common goal.

The SOUND of the experience changes as you leave the shore and make progress. The different accents, high-pitch squeals of children, excitable and sometimes nervy laughter from some, as you all get under way. Then it calms down, and you hear the sounds of nature: gulls wheeling across the Bay, the haunting sound of the oystercatcher, the plaintive cry of a curlew, the chattering of a flock of starlings, ready to mass over the Silverdale reed beds just before dusk. It's all wonderful to behold and to hear.

The human volume then rises once again at the excitement of nearing 'the crossing.' Everyone lines up on the bank of the Kent, and on a given signal from the Guide, you start to cross, with splashes and swishes of swirling water, usually up to your knees. Then the long home straight up the sand bar, over the muddier ditches and dykes of the salt marsh, along the railway embankment

SAFE CROSSING: Charity fundraisers step out into the flowing waters of the Kent Channel, halfway into their cross-bay walk.

LEADERSHIP, 'MOSES'-STYLE: Cedric guides his 'flock' across the 'Wet Sahara' of Morecambe Bay, walking the eight miles from Arnside to Kents Bank.

and over the level crossing to Kents Bank Station.

The SMELLS of the Bay are also there to savour and to breathe in. The freshness of the sea-salted air is uppermost. No petrol fumes, or industrial pollution, invades your sanctuary in the Bay. The TASTE of salt is there when you near the open stretches of water, enhanced by the odd bit of chocolate, or the statutory block of Kendal Mint Cake, or a slurp of spring water from your bottle. All part of the unfolding experience. And, of course, the TOUCH sensation of feeling sand in your toes, of pushing against water in the main channel, of walking barefoot over the grass and salt marsh at the Kents Bank side, even the sloppy mud of the creeks can be part of the offering, though many opt for old footwear at this stage.

Part of the unfolding delight en route is the company you meet. Falling into conversation with complete strangers, all thrown together as you stride on. And all human life is there. A lady with a shopping bag, could be going to the Co-op for a loaf of bread. A man in a tweed suit with his trousers rolled up above his knees. Singles, couples, families, organised groups. The outdoors brigade are ever present, up and ready for the challenge. Last week Helvellyn and Striding Edge, this week Morecambe Bay, next week Ingleton Falls, then on with the plans for the Pennine Way. The butcher, the baker, the candlestick maker – all there, and in good heart.

And finally, after eight or nine miles of achievement, it's all over. A chat with Cedric and his family, and the new guide Michael; a tea or coffee at Abbot Hall Hotel; and, of course, the welcome relief of a toilet. Back home by coach, or by train, many leaving at Arnside, where they have left their car. For me, no walk is complete without fish and chips, a fitting finale to 'a grand day out,' as Wallace and Gromit would have it.

Not to be sacrilegious, but some have described Cedric as a kind of 'Moses of Morecambe Bay,' leading his 'children' to a Promised Land of discovery and wonder, giving them safe passage across

FAITHFUL FRIENDS: Cedric's helping hands and assistants on his cross-bay walks. From left to right – Stephen Clarke, 'Tractor John' Barber, John Holland, Lindsay Sutton, Cedric himself, and Rick Worsey. (Inset left – Jonathan Trevorrow and wife Avril, and inset right – Mike Carter).

the often-treacherous sands. The Biblical distance across the Red Sea was said to have been been nine miles long, which is almost the same distance the walk has to take to avoid the shifting and dangerous quicksands. Not that the waters ever part for Cedric: he is far from being Messianic, but he is a leader, with a quiet authority. He would not thank you for the parallel, but like Moses, he always carries a staff or long walking stick. Maybe the Pied Piper of Hamelin might be a better analogy.

Naturally, umpteen celebrities have been guided across the sands, but the truth is that the walk is for Jo and Joanne Public, ordinary folk with a sense of purpose and a will to raise funds for a favourite charity. When Cedric started out back in 1964, between 30 and 40 walkers joined him. Nowadays, the average is nearly ten times that number, amounting to an estimated 10,000 walkers a year.

Help, I need somebody

WITH such numbers come greater requirements, and the need for tried and trusted volunteer helpers has been vital, and much appreciated by Cedric. Over the years, the personnel involved has changed, just like the configuration of the Bay itself. However, some things do not change: Cedric is the boss, safety is paramount, and learning the ropes is important before taking on any kind of mantle.

For years, Mike Carter was a stalwart, a long and trusted helper who has, unfortunately, had to take a back seat through health considerations. 'Tractor John' – John Barber to Grange folk – has used his skills in the vehicle department, and as a former lorry driver, to keep Cedric's old tractor up and running, driving Cedric down to Humphrey Head of late, before he takes over to venture onto the sands, either for a recce before the weekend walks, or to cross the Bay, with a final check, before meeting up with the walkers to lead them off from White Creek.

With his hernia operation, Cedric has relied on others to take the walkers from Arnside to meet up with him and his helpers, Rick Worsey, Stephen Clarke and 'Tractor John.' More often than not, that walk to the coast has been down to John Holland, who has known Ced for more than 25 years. He met him during a walk, back in the days when he and his wife had a caravan on a site at Holker, near Cark and Flookburgh. John, a businessman and consultant who has worked at Barrow for BAE, says: "Cedric encouraged me to join Mike Carter as his 'wingman' for the walk. One thing led to another, and here I am still doing it, as and when I can." Of late, Jon Trevorrow, and his wife Avril, have helped out as volunteer helpers, learning the ropes from an 'Old Master.' For 16 years, Jon worked as crew member, mechanic and navigator on St Anne's lifeboat, south of Blackpool, so he knows the Bay well. Now that he and Avril, a chemist and food scientist, have moved to Grange, they want to help out from this side of the Bay.

For many years, retired businessman Barry Keelan was one of Cedric's assistants, coming out from the Grange side of the Bay. Eventually, the pull of children and grandchildren led him and his wife Jane to return to their native Cheshire.

More recently, walker and sailor Rick Worsey, who sails a small yacht in the Bay, has taken the important role as Cedric's loyal assistant from the Grange shore. Rick, who comes from the Midlands, was involved in outdoor education for many years, and then became a teacher in design technology and latterly Head of IT. He has always loved the South Lakeland and Morecambe Bay area, and he and his wife Denise chose to move to Grange as a halfway house between his son in Peebles and his daughter in Manchester. Once he met Cedric, there was no turning back, and he is now one of the helpers, coming out with Cedric and helping to lead the happy throng 'home' to Kents Bank.

Finally, there is Morecambe-based Stephen Clarke, who Cedric helped train up as a fisherman, and whose full story is told elsewhere in this book. Then there is me, "the guy who writes," assistant to the assistant when time allows, and long-term friend of Cedric and Olive. We all do our bit for Cedric and the cause. Long may it continue as Ced passes on the baton to Michael.

Cedric Robinson MBE is a warm, humorous and very knowledgeable man who has done so much to help Galloway's support blind and partially sighted people across Lancashire.

For most of our staff and volunteers, the name Cedric Robinson will always be associated with our flagship fundraising event, The Morecambe Bay Walk.

For more than thirty years, Cedric has lead tens of thousands of people fundraising on behalf of Galloway's safely across the Bay.

Many of our walkers are blind or partially sighted and being able to take part in the event has helped them to build confidence and feel empowered. There have been many memories made and friendships forged on our walk and Cedric forms a large part of those memories.

The walks have raised over £1 million for Galloway's since they began. This incredible amount has been used to help thousands of people who have been affected by sight loss and none of this would have been possible without Cedric's expert knowledge.

Cedric's support for Galloway's has not been limited to the Morecambe Bay Walks. He has also shown his kind spirit by hosting several fundraising evenings and he also officially opened our Brew Me Sunshine Café in Morecambe.

We are so grateful to Cedric for his dedication and his continued support for Galloway's over the years.

Emma Russ,
Fundraising and Communications Manager,
Galloway's.

Cedric and the 'Swinging Sixties'

IT was called the 'Swinging Sixties' – an era that spawned the Beatles, the Rolling Stones, and Fleetwood Mac, and across the Pond, Bob Dylan, the Byrds, and the marvels of Motown.

No one was immune during those heady days of long hair, of psychedelic flower power, frilly shirts and bell-bottom trousers, with tinkling bells attached. But Cedric had more on his mind, having a wife and five children to look after – four of them left fatherless when Olive's first husband died at a young age. For Cedric, there were no Parka-wearing Lambretta trips to Morecambe, or joining the motorbike brigade for a Rockers' reunion in Blackpool. He did have quite a fashionable quiff in those days, and his wife did wear mini-skirts in her day: after all, the beautiful, blue-eyed Olive was a former Miss Leeds in her youth.

But the 'swing' Cedric was most interested in was the 'Big Band Swing' music knocked out by Flookburgh Brass Band, in which he played a mean trombone. The other 'swing' – far more important to his livelihood as a fisherman – was the swing of the River Kent Channel across the estuary.

In the autumn of 1963, when 30-year-old Cedric moved into Guide's Farm, ready to start leading walks as the Queen's Guide to the Sands the following spring, the River Kent channel was right up against Grange-over-Sands' Promenade and its famous seafront Lido. It's hard to believe nowadays as you look out from Kents Bank Station onto a huge expanse of marsh pasture, but back then, it was a rock-strewn shoreline right up to the railway embankment, the Kent channel running adjacent to Humphrey Head, just along the coast.

From Cedric's new home – looking out over the Bay, between Grange and Kents Bank – a fifty-yard drive across the railway

GETTING THE MEASURE OF THE BAY: Lancaster's 'First Lady' Dr Ada Pringle has monitored the channel changes of the Kent Estuary for more than fifty years.

level crossing led straight to that rocky shoreline. On the other side of the Bay, at Silverdale and Hest Bank, acre after acre of salt marsh stretched out, untouched by the River Kent. Over Cedric's 55 years as Guide, all that has changed dramatically – and Lancaster University coast specialist Dr Ada Pringle can verify that scientifically.

Dr Pringle – "Call me Ada, everybody does" – has been monitoring the activity involving the Kent Estuary since those dramatic, channel-swinging Sixties, right up to the present day. Ada carried out specific monthly measurements along the Silverdale Salt Marsh between 1984 and 2010, and reveals: "By then, the kilometre-wide marsh of 1975 had gone to nothing. A whole kilometre of salt marsh was virtually eroded away in 35 years."

Her scientifically-recorded findings act as 'the Bible' for coastal and channel changes in Morecambe Bay, and they come with the authority of a coastal geomorphologist of great repute and standing. She is now 82, and an Honorary Research Fellow at Lancaster University's Environment Centre, and is referred to as 'Lancaster's First Lady,' an unofficial title given to her since she was the first female academic to be employed at the new university, when it was founded back in those Swinging Sixties.

Ada, who is also an expert on Spurn Point at the mouth of the River Humber on the North Sea coast, recalls doing an extended Morecambe Bay walk back in the day when she was a young tutor at Liverpool University, before her move to the new Lancaster campus in 1964. She says: "It was in 1963, just after Cedric had taken on the post of Guide. A small group of students and myself walked from Ulverston's Canal Foot to the Cartmel Peninsula, then travelled by coach to Kents Bank, and from there to Hest Bank by foot. We did it at tremendous speed before the tide came in. As the new guide, Cedric was concerned that we made good progress and we did. But what is uppermost in my mind is that the shingle shoreline at Kents Bank was right by the station, with the channel just a short distance away – and it was the same at Humphrey Head. That same year, there was turf cutting on the marsh at Silverdale. By 2010, there was little of that marsh left. It had been eroded by the channel swinging across the estuary to the eastern side."

Irrespective of any consideration of climate change and its possible effects on the Bay, Ada says: "The movement from shore to shore of the Kent Channel is the natural swing over time. It had been close to the Silverdale shore before. It moved near to the limestone cliff in 1915, leaving a foot-high marsh 'cliff' in front of it. Then the channel started to move west towards the Grange shore and a new salt marsh began to develop in front of the 1915 marsh cliff, eventually becoming a whole kilometre wide. Then, in 1975, when the channel moved east again, the erosion of the salt marsh started once more, eventually penetrating to the limestone cliff. I think

SWALLOWED BY THE SANDS: A four-by-four vehicle used by cocklers, and which became stuck in quicksand, is revealed eight years or so on, after the River Keer changed its channel off the Morecambe side of the Bay. Today, it is back under the sands again. (Picture by Phil Forster)

that pattern will recur."

Whilst the Silverdale marsh was eroding from the mid-1970s onwards, on the opposite western side, a marsh was beginning to form off Kents Bank during the 1980s, and spartina grass began to appear. By 1991, Ada confirms that it was almost continuous meadow in places. Nowadays, it's a complete marsh, with creeks where streams run. However, from 2007 onwards, the channel had swung west again, and began to erode that new marsh on the Grange side – and that continues to this day. At Kents Bank, the marsh which had extended to more than one kilometre wide is now only about half that width. Ada sees the channel swing across the estuary as "down to natural processes," adding: "It is not man-made or man-caused."

Who knows? We may yet see vessels sailing in to Grange Promenade, just as the tourist steamers did in yesteryear: trips across the Bay from the old pier at Morecambe to the long-gone pier near Grange Lido.

We would like to extend a heartfelt thank you to Cedric Robinson MBE, for the fabulous walks he has led our supporters on for the past 10 years.

The Morecambe Bay Walk has become a regular and much-loved fixture in the East Lancashire Hospice Calendar of Events attracting people from all over our area to participate.

The Walks have helped us to raise in excess of £75,000, which is an absolutely fantastic amount.

Every year we need to raise £3.7 million to continue to provide free, expert, patient-centred care and support for patients and their families.

This is not an easy task, especially for a small local charity, so we are very grateful for Cedric's support over the years. A huge thank you once again to Cedric Robinson and we wish him and his family all the very best.

Jennifer Quinn,
Corporate Fundraiser,
East Lancashire Hospice.

Cast your net on the other side of the Bay

SAND and water are in Stephen Clarke's blood.

At the tender age of seven, he went out exploring the sands with his brother – and that sparked a life-long love of the wide-open expanses of Morecambe Bay.

Many years earlier, it had been the same with Cedric, who joined his father as a horse and cart 'fisherman' from the age of fourteen.

For Stephen who was born and brought up on the Morecambe side of the Bay, those early days of discovery and exploration would sow a seed that would germinate fully more than forty years later.

Little did Stephen realise that one day the 'King of the Bay' would become a trusted friend, and something of a fishing father figure, tutoring Stephen in the tried-and-tested arts and crafts of 'fishing by foot.'

Naturally, as a Morecambe lad – a 'Sand grown 'un' – who was born within sight of the sea, you'd think Stephen's connection with water would be with the vast volume out there in the Bay. However, the 'water in Stephen's blood' turned out to be the stuff we drink. For more than 30 years, he worked for North West Water, then for United Utilities.

In his spare time, Stephen always enjoyed regular fishing trips on the edge of the Bay just to the north of Morecambe. He would often go out at the crack of dawn if the tide was early, and then after work, depending when the next tide occurred. He never thought he would become devoted to the pursuit, albeit as 'a full-time amateur,' until a water industry colleague came up to him 14 years ago and told him the company were looking to make redundancies from inspector-level employees. Stephen grabbed his chance to turn his fishing activities from being a sideline to an

NET RESULT: Morecambe Bay foot fisherman Stephen Clarke checks out his nets near Priest Skear off Hest Bank. (Picture by Phil Forster)

everyday pursuit – a labour of love that put fish right up there on the menu for his family and friends.

Seeking to learn the ins and outs of Bay fishing, there was only one man to turn to for his expertise, knowledge and his willingness to help. Stephen, now 67, and thoroughly enjoying his outdoor life, explains: "Cedric is such a nice fellow. When I rang him and explained what I wanted to do, he said: 'Well, you'd better come round and see us.' That's just what I did. I spent a whole season going out on the sands with him. I brought a net round to Guide Farm, where Cedric lives on the Grange side of the Bay, and he took me out from near Humphrey Head and taught me the tricks of the trade, right down to the art of properly looping the rope round the fishing net posts set in the sand.

"In return, I would supply him with hazel posts that had been coppiced in Silverdale. They were only 50 pence apiece, but he recognised that I wanted to thank him and that I appreciated his time and effort to turn me into a fisherman. Now, I go out after every tide off Red Bank, on the Morecambe side of the Bay, and put into practice everything I learned from him. I thought I could fish before I went out with Cedric, but I learned better. He taught me such a lot. After all, Ced's been going out on foot, then with horse and cart, then by tractor, for more than 70 years. Such a wealth of knowledge and experience – and he's helped pass it on to me. I feel honoured to be part of the Bay fraternity."

Like all folk who live round the shores of the Bay, Stephen has always had the greatest respect for the tides, the currents, the shifting channels, and the speed with which things can change. As he says: "Cedric reinforced the thought that should always be in the back of your mind: 'The tide comes in faster than a galloping horse.'"

Stephen's childhood fascination with the Bay was given a boost in 1963 when he did his first Bay walk, before Cedric was installed in the office of Queen's Guide. As Stephen explains: "It was from Hest Bank to Grange in those days and two guys did it – one guide took the party to the River Kent, the other took them through the

SHORE THING AT SILVERDALE: The row of cottages on the Silverdale coast looks out over the retreating sea, leaving a sandy bay fringed by exposed rocks.
(Picture by Paul Nickson)

river channel, which could be quite fierce, and on from there.

"The speed of the water in a channel can be up to five or six knots, nearly 7 miles per hour. I know how hard a tide can be too. I nowadays use 8ft scaffolding poles instead of hazel cuttings, and I've found them bent like bananas. The four feet of rod buried down in the sand are fine, but the four feet above are bent by the power of the water. Admittedly, that's when the nets are hung between the poles, and the debris on them makes them like a wall against the tide, but it leaves you with a feeling for the power of nature. When you walk through a fast-flowing channel, I learned very quickly that you walk across sideways to the water flow. If you turn, and face the flow with your full body, you expose a greater area of resistance, and you can lose your footing and be swept away down the channel."

But he adds: "I don't want to frighten people off doing the cross-bay walk. Cedric would never expose people to those conditions. He has instilled in me the message: "Safety first. A fisherman can sometimes take a risk or make a misjudgement. It can happen. But where walkers are concerned, you must eliminate the element of risk as much as possible."

Stephen, who has had a fishing permit for 20 years now, insists he has never had any thought of becoming a commercial fisherman, adding: "I love the Bay, and it's a bit like having an amateur hobby with professional standards. As long as I can keep the larder full, have a fresh fish diet, and provide some for my friends, including Cedric, I'm happy."

He's learned, and been taught by Cedric, to 'read' the Bay, keeping the nets in one place for as long as possible. "It can be a long and laborious process moving three hundred feet of nets and the poles to a new position in a new channel. It all depends on where the River Keer and the River Kent move to. Sometimes your nets can be left high and dry after a few weeks, though it can be up to nine months on the side of the same channel."

There are definite seasons for different fish – winter for cod, springtime for Dover sole, summer and autumn for plaice, bass and mullet. He respects the need for conservation of stock, with a current restriction on bass being in place, the allowance being one sea bass allowed per person per day. Other fish have now returned after conservation measures. As Stephen says: "Any unwanted species are returned into the channels to live on."

Stephen can look back to the time it all began for him when he and his brother did 'set lining' or 'long fishing' as youngsters. He recalls: "We had a long piece of string with loops on it. We attached hooks to the loops and set them up on branches by the nearest channel to shore. I still remember the excitement of going there after the tide had gone out and seeing a plaice caught in a hook. That kept our mum happy with us too. We had to gut them, and she cooked them for us. An early taste of fishing and its rewards."

Stephen's morbid discovery of Chinese cockler's skull

STEPHEN Clarke will never forget the unfolding horror of the Chinese cocklers' disaster in the Bay.

On a winter's night in February, 2004, 23 Chinese men and women were swept out to sea as they harvested cockles against a rising tide. The human tragedy affected everyone associated with the Bay, and led to legislation to outlaw the exploitation of vulnerable people, setting up an independent authority to regulate all aspects of the cockling business.

But for Stephen, the disaster became even more personal when, six years on, he discovered the skull of a female victim half buried in the sand off Silverdale Point. Equally powerful and poignant was another discovery by Stephen almost nine years to the day of the tragedy. Just off Priest Skear, south of Silverdale, he came across a pile of short-handled rakes used by the cocklers on that tragic February night.

"It's a bit morbid really, but I'm 99 per cent sure that the rakes were the ones used by the Chinese cocklers," Stephen said. "Most British cocklers use what we call jumbo boards which you stand on and rock to bring the cockles to the surface. It would appear that the Chinese cocklers simply raked the cockles from the sands. The Chinese are of smaller stature than the British and the rakes I discovered were shorter than normal. It would point to them being used by the Chinese cocklers that fateful night."

There is no doubt about the skull's authenticity. Subsequent DNA tests proved it was that of Liu Qin Ying, a 37-year-old mother whose husband also died in the tragedy. Stephen knew it would be that of a victim as soon as he set eyes on it. "I saw what looked like a set of false teeth upside down in the sand," he reveals. "I went to pick them up and I saw they were attached to something. So, I carefully dug around the object and then realised it was a very small skull . . . and the teeth were very, very perfect, so it was obviously a young person."

The victim's husband, 37-year-old Yu Hua Xu, also perished that night, leaving their 13-year-old son Zhou orphaned, back in China. Just one of the Chinese cockle-pickers remains unaccounted for, with the body of Dong Xin Wu still missing.

The deaths exposed a shady world of cheap labour in which vulnerable migrants were exploited by human traffickers and criminal gangs. Gangmaster Lin Liang Ren, who sent the cocklers out on to the sands, was given a 14-year prison sentence for manslaughter.

The disaster unleashed one of the biggest police operations that the Lancashire force has ever handled, with officers despatched to China to verify victims and claims.

But as Stephen concludes: "A fund was started for the orphan Zhou, and enough money was raised to help with his care and later to send him to university. It's a heartening end to a story of unfolding and needless tragedy."

To the Victims of Morecambe Bay

From a distant land they came
To pluck the riches of the Bay
But many would be lost before
The dawn of the following day.
The swollen rivers from the flood
Had added to the tide,
Unannounced it stole around
As the lonely curlew cried.
Lulled by the silent calm
They worked the cockle seam
Remembering their families
As in a distant dream.
Terrible was the Bay's deceit
And as the tide drew near
In terror they finally realised
Their Armageddon was here.
The sirens of the sands beseeched
With beauty, wild and free, and
Those beguiled could not believe
The treachery of the sea.
Wearily the men who came to save
Watched the breaking of the day
Powerless to change the terrible night
That had occurred on Morecambe Bay.

Sue Wilkinson,
Formerly of Cart Lane, Grange-over-Sands.
2004

Cedric Robinson MBE was appointed as the Queen's Guide to the Sands in 1963. Coincidentally, the same year saw the RNLI introduce the first of their D Class inshore lifeboats. Affectionately remembered by a generation of children as 'Blue Peter lifeboats', they are fast, manoeuvrable, relatively light and requiring little depth of water. For the first time the charity had in its fleet a rescue craft that was suited to the navigational challenges and conditions posed by Morecambe Bay and so in 1966 the RNLI opened Morecambe lifeboat station; beginning the 50-year relationship between Cedric and its volunteer crews.

Fundraising in aid of the RNLI

Cedric has visited Morecambe's RNLI lifeboat station, and more recently its inshore rescue hovercraft station, on numerous occasions over the years. Regarded by crew members with an affection and respect verging on awe, he has over the years been unstintingly generous with his time and support for the life-saving charity in two distinct ways.

Firstly, due to the decline of the local fishing industry, Morecambe's lifeboat volunteers are now almost exclusively drawn from non-maritime backgrounds. Cedric's willingness to give advice and share his knowledge and experience, with those who have the sense to heed it, has been operationally invaluable. As has his work in publicising the dangers that Morecambe Bay poses to the unwary or ill-prepared.

Financially, Cedric has supported the RNLI by leading an annual, fundraising cross-bay walk; enabling the organisation to raise thousands of pounds.

In an age when the term 'local legend' seems much overused; to those living, working and playing in and around Morecambe Bay, with regard to Cedric Robinson, it is entirely appropriate.

Colin Midwinter,
Press Officer, Deputy Launching Authority and Visits Officer.
RNLI

Birds, bees, bugs . . . and Eric Morecambe!

WHEN it comes to nature's numbers game, the figures are quite staggering.

More than a quarter of a million birds come to Morecambe Bay every year – many passing through on their winter migration journey, many staying for the winter, while others live here permanently or choose to stay.

Some of them opt for the reclusive way of living, preferring to keep a low profile, while hiding out in the Bay area reed beds, which are the largest in the North West. Other birds are communal, putting on mass-participation 'shows,' ready to be observed by the human population that live in the Bay area, or who are visiting the surrounding shores.

It is almost beyond belief that up to 200,000 starlings can take part en masse in their 'murmuration' spectacular as they wheel and turn, almost as one, over the reed beds of RSPB Leighton Moss Nature Reserve near Silverdale. For once, the word 'awesome' is apposite, as the starlings put on their seemably-choreographed display of aerobatic skill, just before dusk during the autumn and winter months.

Cedric feels blessed to have witnessed the wonder of wildlife in the Bay over his 'watch' as both fisherman and Guide. He says: "You can't help but be moved, even thrilled, by the wildlife, especially the birds. It's comforting in a funny sort of way to be walking out and seeing such large numbers gathering as a flock on a far sandbank, then seeing them fly off all together as the tide floods over and submerges the bank.

"I particularly like the sound of oystercatchers. They're so distinct and beautiful, with their black and white plumage and their long,

PRESERVE THE RESERVE: Morecambe Bay area's invaluable feeding, resting and breeding sanctuary at Leighton Moss, near Silverdale.

bright orange bills. I'm told that nearly half of all Europe's oystercatcher population flies into Britain for the winter months – and Morecambe Bay gets its fair share of them. I suppose the downside is that they eat a lot of cockles and mussels. As long as there are plenty left for us fishing folk, I'm ok with that. But overall when you learn that more than 250,000 birds live in and around Morecambe Bay during winter, it's a staggering number. It shows how important the Bay is for birdlife."

Certainly, at Leighton Moss, the feel-good factor is there in abundance. When you wander round the reserve, or look out over the Bay, or take in the images and information from the displays in the Leighton Moss cafe, your love of nature and all its marvels is enhanced immensely.

However, there are threats, fears and warnings that need to be heeded too, when it comes to the environment we live in . . . and Morecambe Bay is no exception.

Climate change, sea invasion, food fluctuations, 'coastal squeeze' and 'flights of fear'

LEIGHTON MOSS warden Richard Miller warns that the number of birds in the Bay is declining and he points to a number of factors coming together to cause this worrying trend. Certainly, he knows what he is talking about. He graduated in Zoology at Aberdeen University, then spent six months as a Leighton Moss volunteer, before working for the RSPB at other sites. Back he came to Lancashire, and now in his late thirties, he has been in the top job at the reserve for the past 12 years.

He says candidly: "Climate change is perhaps the major concern. With general global warming, birds from the cold northern climes don't need to fly as far south for the winter. So the bottom edge of their range is clipped off, and that can mean Morecambe Bay gets less wildlife visitors. Sea level rises, which is a growing trend, means that erosion of the coast is an issue too. Our salt marshes around the Bay are vulnerable and that has implications for birdlife, for roosting and for food resources – and that is the third element, the supply of food in the Bay itself.

"In the past, there has been a decline in cockle beds through over-fishing, with the knock-on effect of less young cockles for future stocks. With less food available, the birds move on. Fortunately, things are getting better now, with more regulation and bans on cockling at certain times when the threat is high. That is a heartening development, and is in everyone's interest, including the professional cocklers who depend on the Bay for their livelihood, now and in the future."

Richard adds: "The final threat factor to birdlife is what we call 'the coastal squeeze' and 'flights of fear.' More and more people are moving to live on the coast, and the number of visitors is increasing too. That is a good thing for raising people's interest in wildlife and coastal issues, but it can put a squeeze on the coast, and bring pressures and disruption for birds in their natural habitats. Unless visitors are discerning where and how they go, it can mean less places where birdlife is happy to roost and live. When they are scared and fly away, we call it 'flights of fear.' It means lots of wasted energy for them, and that can affect their well-being and survival.

"We welcome people discovering the Bay and its surrounds, and Cedric's walks have done just that, but you need areas where birds can be left alone. Leighton Moss and the marshes in front of us provide that habitat, mainly because they are inaccessible and not over-developed."

Pollution, plastic and nurdles

BOTH Cedric and Richard are concerned at the effects of general pollution in the oceans, in our atmosphere, and in the Bay in particular, though Richard stresses that with river clean-ups and less coastal dumping in the Bay, there are signs of some improvements in sea water quality.

However, Richard adds: "What we call 'the plastic burden' is evident, and it is a worry. Most people observe the usual plastics washed up, such as plastic bags or larger solid objects, but when you have a more trained eye and an increased awareness, you can spot a real danger on the shores of the Bay, in the form of 'nurdles.' It may sound an odd word, but it's the term scientists use for extremely-small plastic pellets – the size of a lentil. They are washed in on the tides, and they represent a real threat to wildlife and sea life."

Like Richard and his RSPB colleagues, scientists fear that nurdles are the hidden pollutant that often go unnoticed. Even Cedric is aware that it's "the hidden pollution, the stuff you can't see," that represents a threat to the future of the Bay's healthy existence. Marine scientists point out that nurdles are so small that they go undetected, but can have a big effect on delicate sea life and the ocean's ecosystems if they enter the food chain. They point out that nurdles also attract background pollutants like the pesticide DDT and PCBs – full name, polychlorinated biphenyls – which are potentially harmful to wildlife and humans alike. Restrictions and bans may now be in place to halt the use of these toxic chemicals, but in 2017, a post-mortem on a killer whale, that died off Tiree in the Inner Hebrides, revealed it contained more than a hundred times the level that scientists say will have organic consequences. The waters of Morecambe Bay are just 300 miles or so south of Tiree.

There may be cause for concern, but Richard and his staff also stress the positives, the advances and the achievements that are being made.

Always look on the bright side of life

WITH the mantra: 'Always look on the bright side of life,' there are massive pluses, with RSPB Leighton Moss, and Morecambe Bay, being at the heart of the action. Around 100,000 visitors beat a path to the reserve each year, and through the centre's education programmes, thousands of visitors, particularly children, are learning their birdlife ABC, and more. From the astonishing avocets to bashful bitterns to cheerful chiffchaffs, visitors learn about nature and how to distinguish one species from another.

Richard highlights the proud story of the return of the avocet, a wading bird with its distinctive curved-back bill. This happened back in 1997, before his time in charge, but so proud are the RSPB of their success that the avocet is the branded emblem of the organisation. The bird was extinct as a breeding bird in the UK by 1840, but after the war a few visited the Suffolk coast. One of Richard's predecessors, John Wilson, is on record as saying: "One of my proudest achievements is that we've attracted avocets back to Morecambe Bay by transforming an over-grazed area of salt marsh into the wildlife-rich pools you see today."

By 2002, the avocets were breeding in the Bay area again, and

Richard adds: "We are heartened by this development. There are some good years, some bad, but the avocet is a long-living bird and if a pair have two or three chicks every alternative year, it's a success."

Then there is the 'booming bittern.' Quite naturally, Richard and his colleagues are excited about this unfolding success story. He explains: "For ten long years, there was no bittern breeding nest on the fringes of Morecambe Bay. We purposefully improved and extended the reed beds, and rejuvenated them as a way to attract more birdlife, including the bittern. In 2018, it paid dividends when we heard the boom of the bittern and saw nesting take place. Our hope is that the male will return. The species is a migrating one, the birds flying in from Eastern Europe, and they are very difficult to monitor because they arrive and leave at night. In springtime, when they leave, they fly up into the air and muster together before flying off over Lancashire and Yorkshire and over the North Sea. We are concentrating on making the reserve an attractive and productive place to entice them to breed again. That is what we are working on."

Certainly, the avocet and bittern stories have captured the public's imagination . . . and so has the success of the Morecambe Bay starling population, with their majestic and signature 'murmurations.' Richard explains that by extending and renovating the reed beds, up to 200,000 starlings are roosting at Leighton Moss, adding: "They rarely roost on the same reed twice, so renewal is vital. They huddle together for warmth and mutual protection. They set off en masse in the mornings, splitting up for eating purposes, and they dive and swoop together en masse as the sun is going down, before diving on to the reeds. It is an amazing sight for all to see on the shores of Morecambe Bay. Of course, such a mass collection of small birds attracts the marsh harrier – we have six at the moment – and the barn owls who pick them off wherever possible. That's nature for you."

Cedric, who first visited Leighton Moss shortly after it opened,

took a party of local birdwatchers and bird reserve helpers across the Bay at the time. Naturally, he has a 'bird story' to tell. He recalls: "Many years ago, when my father was still fishing, I was setting off cockling with my daughter Jean. We were going down the tracks and suddenly saw a large bird in front of us. It was a greylag goose and it wouldn't move. Maybe it was tired from its long flight south from the Arctic area, or maybe it wasn't well. Amazingly, it allowed me to pick it up. I put it in the fish box, went cockling, brought it back and gave it to my dad. He kept poultry, and the goose lived quite happily with the hens and came to eat with them every morning when they were fed. My old dad grew quite fond of it. Then, one day, after 12 months of free eating, it flew off and we never saw it again. As my dad said: "The ungrateful b----r!""

Eric, Ernie and other birds of a feather

OLDER hands get a kick out of being in the Eric Morecambe Hide, many being somewhat surprised that the great comedian from across the Bay in Morecambe itself, has a birdwatching shelter named after him. It's not that well known, but Eric was a keen observer of wildlife, particularly birdlife, from his youthful days, growing up in his home town on the coast. In the 1970s and 80s, he was friendly with bird expert and mimic Percy Edwards, who had a guest spot on the Eric and Ernie Show as a result. Percy took all the jokes and gentle jesting in his stride, and even put in his own two penn'orth, making both the illustrious stars laugh out loud with his unscripted comments. Eric, of course, had the last laugh when Ernie affected surprise at a noise overhead, with Eric shooting out the line: "Don't worry, it's only Percy Edwards flying south for the winter."

GRACE, STYLE AND ELEGANCE ON THE WING: The stunning dusk-time spectacle of thousands of starlings in the formation flight of a 'murmuration' on the Morecambe Bay coast, before they roost in the reed beds of Leighton Moss RSPB Reserve.

The reserve was chosen for two years running, in 2013 and 2014, to host BBC's Autumnwatch, with Chris Packham, Michaela Strachan, Martin Hughes-Games being entranced by the birdlife they found. It's testimony too that naturalist Simon King and Welsh nature presenter Iolo Williams regularly drop in.

The Chorley Catenian Association have enjoyed the privilege of walking across the sands with Cedric Robinson MBE for nearly 30 years, raising funds for our President's chosen charities, including Derian House, St Catherine's Hospice, Lancashire TAAG, Rainbow House and The Friends of the Holy Land, to mention just a few.

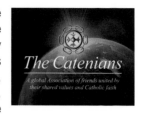

During that time, we have endured dry and wet, hot and windy, shallow and deep, but always in the trust and safety of Cedric, a remarkable man, so knowledgeable whilst at the same time, calm, reassuring and humble, as he talks to walkers throughout these events.

Our walks have started at Arnside and occasionally Hest Bank or Silverdale, but as we arrive at Kents Bank, we are met by Olive, Cedric's lovely wife and soulmate, plus his daughter Jean. Occasionally younger son Paul has accompanied Cedric, taking photographs to use at those winter evening lectures.

In addition to the traditional route, we have also experienced Cedric's walks to Chapel Island and across the Duddon Sands.

So, thank you Cedric for your time and friendship, you are truly the "Knight" of the Sands as well as being a gentleman. We wish you and Olive all the best as you transition into your new Ambassadorial and Advisory role and look forward to visiting you at Guides Farm for many years to come.

John A. Holland,
President,
Chorley Catenian Association.

Well, did you ever?

IT'S one of the most surprising revelations. You don't expect a commercial sea fisherman to admit that he's only been on a boat once in his life – "and that was a nightmare."

Cedric has fished on foot, by horse and cart, and by tractor over the past seven decades or so, travelling right across the 120 square miles of tidal sands that constitute Morecambe Bay. There was never any need for a fishing boat in that kind of terrain. Quite simply, the 'Flookburgh Boys' just thought of boats as unnecessary, superfluous and a complete waste of money.

The term 'sea legs' simply meant having limbs strong enough to walk and wade the three miles or so to the channels in the Bay, where you could set your nets at low tide, then harvest your catch when the tide had come in and gone out once more.

So it was with a good deal of trepidation that Cedric accepted the offer of an expenses-paid trip to the Isle of Man to give a lecture to the Guild of Outdoor Writers. As soon as he arrived at Heysham Ferry Terminal, he knew it might have been unwise to accept the offer, even though it was prestigious and well intentioned. The weather was foul, the Irish Sea was churning, and those who disembarked from the IOM 'Packet' "looked green about the gills."

As Cedric relates: "I should have known better. It was bad weather on land, let alone at sea. Some friends who took us down to Heysham Docks, on the other side of the Bay from our house, asked us to wave to them on shore as we got under way. No such luck. You couldn't get on deck, visibility was poor anyway, and I couldn't get over to a window standing up – and that was just in the harbour estuary.

"It was rough all right. I wasn't seasick, but I didn't feel well at all. When we arrived I had to take myself in hand to give the

lecture, which I just about managed. We then went on a horse and tram at Douglas, and the horse was spooked up by the conditions. It had to be calmed down and removed, rather like me! I tell you, I was happy to get back home – and even more grateful that I was a boat-less fisherman. Those deep-sea trawler men who went out from Fleetwood and Grimsby have my eternal admiration. I'm happy to go by foot in Morecambe Bay."

'The wonderful world, right there on my doorstep'

CEDRIC is certainly not the most travelled man in the world. Most Cumbrians have been to Carlisle, and so has Cedric – "but only the once, mind you." He enjoyed the trip – all 65 miles of it – to receive an honour from the University of Cumbria, and he liked the city itself, but as he adds: "It's a long way north for me, and I have no real reason to visit the place that often."

It's fair to say that Cedric's 'world' is the Bay, with all its richness and its natural attraction. His stories of occasional visits to places as far afield as Lancaster, Morecambe, and even to Leeds, have an old world charm about them. It's almost as though he comes from another era, when a simpler and perhaps less complicated way of life was the natural order. He does have a car, but only uses it to pop down to Grange-over-Sands, to go to Arnside for a cross-bay walk, to judge a sandcastle competition in Morecambe, or to do a weekly shop with his daughter Jean and his wife Olive in Kendal, "the big city." He has been on forays to Windermere in the Lakes, and to Clitheroe in East Lancashire, where he addressed a packed auditorium at the Grand Theatre. But much of the world's

FISHING TO LIVE, LIVING TO FISH: Cedric out in Morecambe Bay tending his nets, as he has done for more than 70 years, following in the footsteps of his father and grandfather before him. (Picture by Paul Nickson)

attractions cannot compete with the wonder of the Bay and its surrounds, and the homely pleasures of his existence at Guide's Farm.

Needless to say, Cedric has never been up in a plane. He reminds you that 40 years ago he was offered the opportunity to appear on a French TV chat show, with all expenses paid, including return flights from London to Paris. He says: "It was a non-starter all round. I've never flown and I don't fancy doing so. When I learned that they wouldn't supply a parachute, I told them I couldn't fulfil the engagement."

Then there was an offer to take him up for an aerial view of the Bay in a helicopter. Ced recalls: "The pilot who made the offer was on one of our cross-bay walks. He was a very well-built man who must have weighed 20 stone. I couldn't help thinking the helicopter would fall to earth with his weight on board, so I politely declined and told him that I'd keep my feet on the ground."

Heart 'n soul of the Bay

WHAT is amazing, and ultimately heartening, is that for all the focus on his immediate surrounds and the routine daily chores of running a smallholding, Cedric is neither small-minded, nor closed off to society and its issues. Nor is he bigoted against anyone from outside his own locale.

That facet of his personality is proved by the story of a medical crisis that came out of the blue. It is a great surprise for many people when they learn that nearly 25 years ago, Cedric had a double heart bypass operation – and thereby lies a revealing tale

TIME AND TIDE WAIT FOR NO MAN: Cedric checks out the tide table at his Guide's Farm home, preparing the timings of the cross-bay walks. (Picture by Paul Nickson)

READY FOR THE OFF! Hundreds of fundraising walkers prepare to set off down the Kent Estuary from Arnside on their eight-mile journey to Kents Bank.

of his attitude to life and to people. As he tells it: "I was as strong as an ox, but with fishing and looking after a smallholding, it was a job to make a living back then. Maybe it was the stress of trying to earn enough to keep body and soul together for me, for Olive and for our five children. Who knows? I got a pain in my arm, but the new doctor said it wasn't a heart attack. It got worse, and I was having to kneel down with the pain, and the sweating. A female doctor was called and she knew straight away that I had had a heart attack. They rushed me to Barrow Hospital, but I insisted on sitting up on the way.

"They decided I had to have an immediate double heart bypass operation at the specialist heart unit down in Blackpool, and that's what happened. However, while I was there, this local patient from the Blackpool area told me: 'It makes me sick that people like you from north of Morecambe Bay use our facilities down here.' I was stunned and disheartened by that remark. What sort of person says that? I lived a couple of hours away and he regarded me as an outsider. That's not the attitude you should have about anyone, is it?"

And that is the revealing point. That is Cedric's attitude and approach to life down to a tee. He may have a micro-focussed existence, but he has a big vision of people. He meets so many, and is receptive and open to what they say. He has interesting conversations with them, about their own experiences and interests, as well as his own. He listens as well as talks. He is always a joy to be with, and he lifts your spirits. He certainly wouldn't ever consider a man from Blackpool to be an undeserving outsider!

Petrified about meeting people

IT may be a further surprise to cross-bay walkers to find out that when Cedric took on the task of Queen's Guide at the age of 30, he was petrified about meeting people from the big, wide world outside Flookburgh. As he says: "I had never been out of the village socially. It was difficult for me at first."

It's fair to say that his willingness and open nature helped him overcome that initial fear of meeting and conversing with educated and experienced people who had seen more of the world at large than he had, coming from a poor background with so-called limited horizons. But, as people from all walks of life will attest, Cedric has an engaging personality – albeit with a low-key approach to life – and an open-book philosophy that is appealing to so many. More than one observer has said: "What you see is what you get," while others have called him "a true and trustworthy friend."

The Duke of Edinburgh . . . "a bit of a grumpy old b----r."

NOW Cedric has always had a critical faculty, combined with a wicked sense of humour and expression that can take you by surprise. Take his story about when he took the Duke of Edinburgh across the Bay in a four-horse carriage. It is well chronicled how proud Cedric was to be asked to guide Prince Philip across the Bay. What is less well known is the story behind the story, about the build up and sequel to the actual event.

As Cedric reveals: "The then Lord Cavendish came to tell me that Prince Philip would like to cross the Bay by horse and carriage, and could I find a safe place for everyone to muster over at Silverdale. I chose an old people's home and grounds where a helicopter could land. There was a man with a red flag who looked like a lollipop man. It was quite comical. Thousands of people were there in expectation of the event. Further down the coast, Prince Philip was preparing for the ride. We went looking for him in the carriage and we were riding round in circles until an equerry shouted: "Over here, Mr Robinson."

"When we met him, I said: 'Could you all please step down while I tell you of the route and the dangers.' Prince Philip lived up to his reputation for being a bit of a grumpy old b----r when he said curtly: 'Hurry up Mr Robinson, we're going to be here all day!' I wasn't going to have that, and stood my ground. I insisted on addressing them about the dangers of the quicksands, advising them to follow me at all times. After all, that's my job, and I didn't want a disaster with the Duke on board.

"So off we went, the two of us with an entourage behind us, and he soon calmed down and asked me lots of questions. He gradually realised how dangerous it was out on the sands, especially when the Coastguards' vehicle went down in the quicksands. But he was angry about the helicopters overhead, especially when the noise jittered the horses. I thought privately that if he got sharp with me

SHOULDERING THE RESPONSIBILITY: A child is carried safely over the Kent Channel as walkers splash their way across the river in the middle of the Bay.

again, I might let him go down in the quicksands too. Now that would have been a story, wouldn't it – but I thought better of it. In fact, once he settled down, we both enjoyed the experience and got on just fine. At the end, going up to the railway crossing at Kents Bank, the Duke was presented with an engraved tankard, and when he asked in vain if there was one for me too, he insisted on giving me his. I think it was his way of thanking me and making up for being short with me at the beginning."

More smoothly, Cedric has met the Queen on several occasions. When asked if he had ever been to London, he replied: "Aye, on two occasions . . . and I popped in to see the Queen both times!" The first occasion was to receive his MBE. Ever honest and forthright, Cedric reveals: "This toff in attendance told me to call her Mam, as in jam. He told me to only speak when spoken to. It

A RIGHT ROYAL CANTER: Cedric accompanies the Duke of Edinburgh in his carriage of four, with its magnificent Cleveland horses. (Picture by Peter Cherry)

TRAPPINGS OF SUCCESS: Carriage riders set off on their journey across the Bay, just as cross-bay travellers would have done before the railway and passable roads were built round the Morecambe Bay coastline.

made me very nervous, and I went as deaf as a stone. I bowed and was trembling when she gave me my gong. I don't know why because I'm not a nervous person. Then, when she said: 'I believe you took my husband across the Bay,' I was alright and had a decent chat with her – but I didn't tell her I had to take him in hand."

'King of the Bay' meets the Queen of the Land

CEDRIC has dined with the Queen on three occasions. The first time was in Lancaster at a Duchy celebration, where Prince Philip was in attendance too. Then Cedric was invited to an event at the Castle Green Hotel in Kendal, where he again met Prince Philip, along with the widow of the comedian Eric Morecambe. Ced is no 'inverted snob,' but he can't help telling it how it is when he recalls: "There were lots of Government officials there. You know the type. They speak with a plum in their mouth, and the amazing thing is that they can speak and eat at the same time."

Finally, he was invited to a function in the Lake District, when he was one of half a dozen people selected to meet the Queen at a luncheon she was attending, along with Princess Anne. Cedric remembers it all too well as he recalls: "I hardly spoke to Her Majesty because she was some distance away, but Princess Anne and myself got on famously. She was so easy to talk to, and, of course, we discussed horses. Both of us have an interest in horses and she wanted to know all about mine."

Cedric also revealed that he would like to meet Prince Charles and maybe take him across. "He seems to care for the environment, like me," said Cedric. "He's interested in nature and the pressures that are in play. I think he would be interested in hearing my views on climate change and the way it seems to be affecting the Bay. I suspect we could have a very interesting exchange of views." He also thinks that "both the boys" – Prince Harry and Prince William – would be interested in doing the cross-bay walk, maybe along

AWAY FROM THE BAY: Cedric and his wife Olive enjoy each other's company at their Guide's Farm home near Kents Bank. (Picture by Paul Nickson)

with their wives. "That would be fun, wouldn't it?" he adds.

All this from a man who was born into the hand-to-mouth existence of a fishing family in Flookburgh. Even when appointed to the post of Queen's Guide, Cedric and Olive still scratched out a meagre living at Guide Farm next to the Barrow–Lancaster railway line. Cedric describes it all with no anger, no rancour, and not a hint of jealousy, as he recalls: "We used to walk along the edge of the railway track to the point where steam trains would spill coal at the bend. We went with a wheelbarrow to collect it for our open fire. I can afford to buy it from a coal merchant nowadays, but that's the way it was for us back then . . . and here we are 55 years on, still warming our feet by that same fire. That's continuity for you."

The open fire is mesmerising as you sit there, listening to Cedric telling his stories, with Olive sitting contentedly in her fireside chair. Cedric's humour is just as warm-hearted. At one point, the cat sat on the outside windowsill, looking plaintively through the glass pane at the rug in front of the fire. I got up, opened the door and the cat walked in. It looked at us, then walked outside to sit on the windowsill again. Cedric looked up at me and said wryly: "It obviously doesn't like the company."

For over a decade the Rosemere Cancer Foundation has been indebted to Cedric Robinson MBE who has provided guided walks over the treacherous sands of Morecambe Bay

for charity walkers. Thousands of Rosemere supporters have been able to complete their crossings safely whilst enjoying the spectacular scenery and surrounds of the Bay.

The walk has been a must-do activity for many thousands of charity fundraisers and supporters across the North West and from further afield. Every year, demand for our charity places has grown, as everyone wants to join Cedric on this spectacular journey across the sands. We've had people from as far afield as Devon and Kent join our walks through family links to the North West.

Cedric has helped the Rosemere Cancer Foundation raise over £100,000 which has made a huge difference for local cancer patients. The monies raised have helped fund many hugely impactful projects and services for the benefit of cancer patients across Lancashire and South Cumbria, ensuring we continue to provide world-class cancer care as close to home as possible for our patients in Lancashire and South Cumbria.

Daniel Hill,
Head of Fundraising,
Rosemere Cancer Foundation.

Cedric's 'Baywatch' . . . technically speaking

PUSHING the boundaries of technology is getting to be routine in Morecambe Bay.

The ebb and flow of the tides, the haunting sound of the oystercatcher on the wing, the vast vistas of open sands may all be a timeless feature of Bay life. Yet, for hundreds of years, man has always wanted to add something else. Depending on your view, the plans for changes have been either exciting enhancements or the equivalent of taking the wrecker's ball to this beautiful citadel of nature, which has been left untouched since the glaciers swept south all those thousands of years ago during the last Great Ice Age.

There have been pressures for change for time immemorial. No doubt the monks on their way to Furness Abbey back in Medieval times harboured their own hopes for a swifter way of travel. They had to endure the long, guided trek by foot or on horseback across the sands from Hest Bank to Kents Bank, then across the Cartmel Peninsula, before the last trek across the Leven Estuary with another guide.

The journey in the 18th and early 19th centuries by horse and carriage could be treacherous, with many deaths being recorded before the railway was built on its circuitous but scenic route around the Bay. It required a short, low viaduct across the Kent at Arnside, a structure that is still being used and admired to this day. What a relief the opening of the Ulverston and Barrow Railway in 1857 was to travellers and to locals along the line. At last, an affordable and safe way to link up to the main West Coast Line from Glasgow to London, then from Carnforth to Yorkshire, and from Preston to Manchester.

Barrage of criticism . . . or of opportunity?

THERE have been seemingly-endless plans to build a road bridge across the Bay to shorten the long and often tedious road journey between Lancaster and Barrow-in-Furness. Allied to this, there has been much talk of using the bridge as a tidal barrage, harnessing the power of the twice-daily tides to create 'green' energy in the form of nature-powered electricity.

Cedric has mixed feelings about such a project, being torn between the need for 'progress' and the conflicting environmental considerations. Honest as ever, he says: "I don't like to see things change, but you can't hold back progress. To a large extent, my life has been at an easy pace, with me in charge of it. Yet around me, the world is moving fast. It may not always be to my liking but that's the way it is.

"The experts have concluded that it was possible to build a barrage and road bridge but that it would be far too expensive. If it ever did come about, there would be advantages, with the clean generation of electricity, but there would be great opposition from the environmentalists. On balance, I'm happy that it was never built. Even so, it keeps being put forward by folk in Barrow and on the West Coast. It is one heck of a road journey right round the Bay at present. On the other hand, there would be a massive impact on birdlife and fishing in the Bay, and the views of the Bay and the surrounding fells and mountains would be affected.

"There will be unexpected consequences too. The tide will scour material on the way in, then deposit silt and sand on the way out, including the areas around the barrage sluices. What are the implications for the upper Bay area too? The tidal range, its nature and its force will definitely change. Has it all been thought through?"

A full test was carried out in the 1980s and Cedric was asked to advise on safety when the drilling rigs were being installed out in the Bay, and he took the gangs out on his tractor. However, he couldn't be there to guide them all the time, and so they brought in an amphibious DUKW, the wartime invention that can travel on land and sea. But as Ced adds: "It seems they thought it could go anywhere in the Bay, and be used for general transport. One day, I looked out and saw that they had loaded it with scaffold from a rig well out in the Bay. All the weight was on the back end, and as they drove towards the shore, the tide was coming in behind them.

"The tidal bore up the Leven hit them and the water came in at the back. They had to throw the scaffolding overboard, and they just made that decision in time. However, the tide then swept the DUKW at great speed on to Chapel Island. They had the fright of their lives. I'm told that one fellow went green with fear. The same type of scenario happened on the Morecambe side when they brought in a crawler machine. They knew the times of the tides, but one site agent always left it to the last minute to come to shore. One time, the tidal bore came rushing in nearly 3 ft high. That gave them a huge fright and they only just made it. Fortunately, the lesson was learned. They found out the hard way that nature is mighty powerful and will have her own way. After these incidents, I gave them a real talking to about the dangers they were playing with. So they made me safety officer and followed my advice and instructions from then on."

Harnessing the wind . . . or tilting at windmills?

WIND turbines have made their entrance to the scene too, with many to be seen nowadays on the skyline off Barrow and the Furness Peninsula.

It's claimed that offshore wind farms are more efficient than those onshore, and there was 'minimal opposition' to the schemes, according to the local paper at the time. They began producing in earnest several years ago, and Cedric says of them: "They don't worry me, because they're well out to sea. But if there were plans to put them in the Bay proper, I would be against them – and, I suspect, a lot of other folk would be too. Not to put too fine a point on it, the move would be catastrophic. The views and the serenity would be lost: they simply don't fit in with what people want from the Bay."

Meanwhile, the West of Duddon Sands Wind Farm – situated ten miles south west of Walney Island, off Barrow – has more than a hundred turbines and cost £1.6 billion to install. This included the laying of undersea power cables to get the electricity to a specially-built sub-station on the Furness Peninsula, which feeds into the UK National Grid. The other farms are the 200 turbines of the Walney Wind Farm and the 30 of the Barrow one – all fed to the Barrow shoreline. All part of the changing coastal scene, and all big business in construction and in production.

It's a real gas out there in the Bay

GAS rigs made their grand entrance from the mid 1980s onwards, and as a major UK source of gas energy, the fields have gone on to supply 15 per cent of the UK's needs. Although two of the fields are called Morecambe Bay North and South, there are others, stretching from the Mersey Estuary to the Barrow offshore area.

Work is still under way to revamp several of the rigs and their pipeline outlets, which promises to unlock a further 3 billion cubic feet of gas, with a grand total of 300 billion cubic feet still under the East Irish Sea as a whole.

It is an amazing development in Cedric's lifetime and his views on the gas-producing rigs are similar to those he holds on the wind farm development. He marvels at the output – at its peak, 15 per cent of UK production, but observes: "I'm glad they are well offshore."

The 'battle' between man and nature

ALL this activity sparked controversy between economic 'progressives' and environmental purists – those who welcomed technological change, warts and all, and those who worried about its effects and its intrusion into the world of nature. Perhaps it was ever thus, but the pace of change and the increase of man-made pollution has heightened the debate, and the scale of what is at stake.

Can man and nature ever live in harmony? Should this 'Wet Sahara,' this haven of nature, be protected from mankind? And what if fracking should ever be seen as a profitable pursuit in the Bay and its surrounds? After all, fracking is already a source of great controversy on the nearby Lancashire plain between Preston and the coast.

Cedric has seen and heard it all over his 70 years in Morecambe Bay, keeping a philosophical and open mind to developments, proposals and suggestions, whilst having his own views too. He says: "The Bay is a very precious place, and very special to me, to the people who live and work here, and to the thousands of visitors who come to the area." One thing is for sure: his 'Baywatch radar' is always switched on.

Rocket Man from the Bay

'ROCKET Man' Steve Bennett may be reaching for the stars with his space quest – but his first stop was Morecambe Bay.

Steve – once a part-time lecturer in space physics at Salford University and now a space entrepreneur – aims to send a reusable rocket to the edge of space, with paying tourists on board.

It's not a fantasy either, with test launches taking place ever since his first attempt from Cartmel Wharf, just off the Ulverston coast, in the Levens Estuary. That was back in the late Nineties and early

2000s, the unmanned launches being successful, apart from the time when the rocket was damaged when it crashed down on to the sands after reaching a height of 5,000 feet.

It's a development that Cedric couldn't have dreamed of when he was a lad growing up in nearby Flookburgh. He says: "On the one hand it was a big surprise that the Bay was getting involved in the space race, but it is the perfect place from a safety point of view. They say that what goes up must come down, and the launch people needed a wide, open area for the landing. It wasn't a surprise that they chose Cartmel Wharf in the Levens Estuary for the launch. It's a high bit of sand bank not far from land. I won't be going up, that's for sure. But just as the cross-bay walks have helped attract a new set of tourists in my lifetime, you never know what it leads to. Arnside to Kents Bank by foot – then up, up and away!"

Ironically, the man succeeding Cedric as Queen's Guide, Flookburgh fisherman Michael Wilson, was asked to take the rocket on his tractor to its launch position on the offshore sandbank. Like Cedric, Michael was unfazed by the request, saying: "Nothing takes you by surprise in this job. You find all sorts out there. Adding a rocket to the tale makes it even more interesting – and it went up and down as planned."

Since that first venture, further experimental launches have been made by Steve Bennett's privately-owned aerospace company, Starchaser, which is based in an industrial unit at Hyde, in the

FROM OPEN SPACE TO OUTER SPACE: Steve Bennett's Starchaser rocket takes off on its experimental launch out on the sands of Morecambe Bay.

Tameside area of Greater Manchester. The company, whose motto is: 'The sky is not the limit,' has the simple aim of being a viable business in space tourism, and to develop a safe, reusable launch vehicle and make a space trip affordable.

Steve, who aims for more test launches from Morecambe Bay, has also been to the Spaceport in the American state of New Mexico, which is a centre used by Sir Richard Branson with his space tourism project. Steve, whose Manchester-based project was backed by a £3 million investment from a benefactor, who wishes to be un-named, says: "Our first Morecambe Bay rocket is on display over there, so they know we mean business." His firm received a €200,000 grant from the European Space Agency, but now mainly depends on finance from the schools outreach programme, which involves education projects in 200 schools a year.

It's a field that is not exactly crowded with competitors, but those with similar dreams of success are pretty big players. Branson has set up Virgin Galactic; electric car entrepreneur and pioneer Elon Musk is well down the track with his SpaceX programme; and Amazon owner Jeff Bezos has his own quest for space stardom in the form of his organisation Blue Origin. With Bezos reputed to be worth a cool $112 billion, the competition for glory and viability is huge.

Yet Steve, who started out as a lab technician with the toothpaste firm Colgate at their old factory near Salford Docks, remains undaunted, and says: "I've met Branson and Musk and I wish them well. The publicity around space tourism has helped change people's attitudes and perceptions. Space tourism is a big pie and there's a lot of space and room out there. It all helps, and it's exciting, but I hope it's accessible too."

In September, 2017, Starchaser's research rocket Skybolt 2 was launched from a mobile platform in Northumberland. The 27ft, unmanned rocket is the largest one ever to blast off from the UK mainland.

Steve's company has linked up with the University of Chester, and has incorporated a project run by Sheffield Hallam University. Now, Starchaser aims to launch a 39ft rocket that has room for one passenger, moving on to develop a three-passenger rocket ship.

The firm even bought 20 acres of land in New Mexico, close to the New Mexico Space Authority site, where Virgin Galactic has its support and administration HQ, but has since sold this.

The commercial race for space is stepping up a gear, with Virgin Galactic making another giant step for Branson after success in December, 2018, with its latest venture. The company launched SpaceShipTwo, VSS Unity, to an altitude of 82,682 metres, the craft being released by a carrier plane at an altitude of 13,000 metres, and reaching a top speed of 2.9 times the speed of sound.

As with everything, there is controversy. Critics say it merely represents 'a high-altitude plane,' not a mission into space. Yet, like Steve Bennett's project, it has caught the imagination. Six hundred people have paid or put down a deposit to fly on Virgin's sub-orbital flights, which will cost $250,000 for a 90-minute out-of-this-world experience.

Branson himself wants to be the first up on the inaugural flight, showing just what Steve Bennett faces in competition – big bucks, big vision and big egos. Will it be a triple whammy for the man who started out his mission in Morecambe Bay?

I have worked for local East Lancashire charities for many years and when the New Year passes my first call is to the Robinson household to arrange the Morecombe Bay Walk.

The sands are a dangerous place, the walk is more arduous than its description, but it is the one challenge of the year that my charity supporters and I really look forward to, secure in the knowledge that Cedric's decades of experience on the sands always produces a safe and well run event. On the day, we are always greeted with a smile as this friendly and personable iconic man holds the audience with his factual and witty tales of the area.

I always like to walk near the back to watch the happy band and listen to the excited banter as over one hundred people snake along a carefully planned route. This year my mind started to wander. I knew of one walker who had already raised over £800. What if everyone here today had raised just a quarter of that? And then what about tomorrow's group? And last week's group? And then mathematical overload kicked in as I knew this had been happening for decades.

Hundreds of thousands? No, millions of pounds raised, countless benefactors and thousands of happy walkers is the legacy of the man who is the 'Sandwalker'.

Denise Gee,
Fundraising Manager,
East Lancashire Hospitals NHS Trust

This other Eden . . . in Morecambe!

WITH the best will in the world, the words 'Morecambe' and 'Garden of Eden' might not appear to sit happily together.

From its heyday as a holiday getaway from the Northern industrial cities, Morecambe went into steep decline, and hit rock bottom soon after the 'Viva España' brigade went abroad on their cheap, sun-seeking package holidays in the 1970s.

Now, nearly 50 years on, there is hope that the old coastal resort could become a born-again 'Paradise on Earth,' as it reconnects with the sea and Morecambe Bay, and embraces ecological and environmental tourism through a bold new venture.

What was good for Cornwall in the biosphere shape of the Eden Project, could now be good for the Lancashire coast. Plans are well down the track to build an £80 million Eden Project North on the site of the closed-down 'Bubbles' swimming pool and its neighbouring, boarded-up Dome Theatre – and the implications for Morecambe and the Bay are massive.

It's calculated that up to 8,000 visitors a day could flock in to visit the site during peak season, reviving the town and surrounding area with a major injection of revenue and renewed purpose. It's estimated that the Eden Project in Cornwall has contributed the staggering sum of £2 billion to the local economy since the state-of-the-art ecological attraction first opened back in 2001. In that time, it's calculated that 20 million people have visited the attraction – and Morecambe Bay folk hope that those figures hold up for them.

But the spin-off is much more than a pounds, shillings and pence calculation. The environmental and educational impact on all those visitors has been profound, with the whole set-up being geared to raising awareness of the beauty of Mother Nature, and by implication, just what is at stake if we do not protect and cherish

FLEXING MORECAMBE BAY'S MUSSELS: Two artist impressions of the planned £80 million Eden Project North, which will take centre stage on Morecambe's seafront, connecting the resort with the Bay. The project is based on Cornwall's Eden Project, which has been a major financial, ecological and educational success story.

our fragile environment.

That is why Morecambe's Eden Project North will not only be by the sea, it will face the sea, and reflect the sea, in the shape of the marine life in Morecambe Bay. With careful thought and awareness, and aiming to reflect its locale, the five huge biospheres planned will be shaped like giant mussels, as though they have been plucked from the Bay itself.

Cedric, who has done his fair share of mussel collecting over his

72 years out in the Bay, approves of Eden Project North's plans to highlight the importance of nature and the Bay. He says: "Basically, we are singing from the same hymn sheet. I tell people on our cross-bay walks about the wonders of nature, and things that are happening in the Bay. I think that the Morecambe project has a similar mission. It all seems to fit together very well."

The designers who have come up with the appropriate mussel theme for Morecambe are Grimshaw Architects, the same company which designed the initial, groundbreaking Cornwall project. It is heartening that partner Jolyon Brewis, who went to Manchester University, says up front: "Morecambe Bay is a truly unique location of outstanding natural beauty. This, in combination with Eden's distinctive approach, will make this a landmark

destination of national and international significance. The aim is to reimagine what a seaside destination can offer – a world-class tourist attraction that is in tune completely with its natural surrounds. We want to connect people with the internationally-significant natural environment of Morecambe Bay, while also enhancing well-being."

It may sound quite lofty for the more homely and humble, little Morecambe of old, but whatever one's mind-set, the ideas are laudable. The revenue raised would all be ploughed back into the Eden Project charity and social enterprise; the educational benefits are not to be scoffed at; and the potential rejuvenation of Morecambe – through revenue, expenditure, jobs and pay – is a given. The case put by the Eden Project is that it has worked once and can surely be made to work again.

The idea is to have both indoor and outdoor experiences at the Morecambe site, the mussel-shaped pavilions housing a variety of environments. Maybe a rainforest and a Mediterranean environment in two of the bio-domes, as is the case in Cornwall, but certainly a marine-focussed one to reflect the Bay just beyond the shoreline beach that the mussels are attached to.

The initial target date for completion in Morecambe is the autumn of 2022. However, now that the feasibility study has been conducted, the emphasis is on raising the funds to make it happen, then to obtain planning permission as soon as possible. Morecambe folk have seen their fair share of false dawns, Noel Edmonds and Mr Blobby among them. However, there are reasons for optimism and hope, in that Eden Project North is based on a proven track record.

It's all part of the vision of Eden Project founder Sir Tim Smit, and of Si Bellamy, Head of Eden International, the spin-off body that is rolling out the 'Eden' social enterprise blueprint in Morecambe . . . and around the world.

Grimshaw Architects are on track to unveil a £150 million scheme at Qingdao in China. There are schemes planned for the Sequoia Forest in California's Sierra Nevada Mountains on the west coast of America; for a symbolic 'resurrection' scheme in earthquake-hit Christchurch in New Zealand's South Island; for an Antarctic insight in an old warehouse area of Tasmania in Australia; while there are three projects planned for the UK.

One is on the River Foyle in Derry, linking three old walled gardens ("one Catholic, one Protestant, one state-owned – we're treading very carefully there," said Sir Tim at the project's launch). Another project, at an advanced stage of planning, promises to be "the best motorway service station in the world" at junction 27 of the M5, linked to Tiverton Parkway. The plan is that visitors will arrive by train and hire electric cars to explore the surrounding countryside. "We're on the cusp of a revolution in transport: within five to eight years I believe all major transport will be electric," says Sir Tim.

Then there's the Morecambe project. The vision is of a seaside resort for the 21st century, and includes "reimagined lidos, gardens, performance spaces, immersive experiences and observatories." Central to this is the series of mussel-inspired pavilions which will house a variety of environments, focussing on marine life and exciting water-related themes.

Si Bellamy emphasises that the project recognises that Morecambe has "a wonderful history of being a place where people come to relax and unwind," adding: "We want to ensure that anything we do enhances the Bay and people's understanding of it and the natural world. This is an opportunity to make a real difference, to connect people with the Bay, a place with unique scientific and natural interest."

Sir Tim stressed that the project had the support of the Lancashire Enterprise Partnership, Lancaster University, Lancashire County Council and Lancaster City Council. He went on: "We're not in the business of building theme parks. We're in the business of building hope, inspiration and leadership. We want to create oases of change, which other people will want to emulate, which then become transformative. We shouldn't be sanctimonious about the problems that face the world. It's not a question of wearing a hair shirt and punishing ourselves. We should be saying: 'Look how cool the world could be.' Our job is to create a fever of excitement about the world, that is ours to make better."

He revealed that with the success of the Cornish centre, he had been bombarded with proposals from Britain and overseas for recreating the Eden effect in other deprived areas. "Mostly they just wanted a Tussauds waxworks with a bolt-on ethical conscience," he said. "That's not our thing."

BRING ME SUNSHINE:
The famous statue of Morecambe's favourite son, comedian Eric Morecambe. The larger-than-life bronze statue stands on the promenade, and offers the perfect picture opportunity to visitors. (Picture by Phil Forster)

Bring Me Sunshine, Morecambe-style

ERIC Morecambe certainly brought a lot of sunshine into people's hearts – and to his hometown.

His statue – in classic 'Bring Me Sunshine' style – stands on the seafront in Morecambe, and is a 'must' stop for all visitors to the resort. They stand by the larger-than-life, bronze sculpture, copying his pose of one hand up above his head, the other behind him, as he does the famous Eric and Ernie song-and-dance routine.

Naturally, visitors sing the words of what became Morecambe and Wise's trademark song as they emulate their favourite comic and have their photo taken. Quite amazingly, visitors spend up to 45 minutes here, enjoying the 'feel-good' experience. Many wonder why Eric has a pair of binoculars round his neck, and are often surprised to find that he was a keen birdwatcher. You can just hear the line: "Oh yes, I'm a keen ornithologist, you know. Don't know what it means, but I am one anyway."

Even the Queen got a buzz from it all when she officially unveiled the sculpure back in 1999 – and, of course, Cedric has a tale to tell about the statue too. He recalls: "Like everyone, I like Morecambe and Wise – not because Eric came from the Bay area, but because together they were one of the finest and funniest acts there has ever been. My connection is that I was invited to an event at the Midland Hotel in Morecambe to meet the sculptor Graham Ibbeson. We were chatting and it turned out he knew about me being the Queen's Guide to Morecambe Bay, and told me he would one day love to do a public statue of me. It's not happened yet, but you live in hope!"

Graham, who has done many public art projects, remembers the conversation only too well . . . and the one Cedric had with his wife. The Barnsley-born sculptor reveals: "He and my wife got on famously. He made her laugh when she told him I had always been interested in the cross-bay walks. He told her: 'Well, I can take him out and leave him there if that's what you want.' She laughed out loud, and made me laugh when she told me. And even though he threatened to let me drown, I'd still like to do a sculpture of him!"

Graham, who is in his late sixties, and who went to London's Royal College of Art, is known as 'The People's Sculptor' for his many and varied commissions of those thought of as 'public heroes.' From his studio in his home town of Barnsley, he made the Laurel and Hardy sculpture, which was unveiled in Ulverston in 2009, the statue being credited with helping to increase tourism in the town by 50 per cent.

In the same way, Eric's statue has helped put Morecambe back on the map. Down the coast in Blackpool, Graham's commissioned sculpture of Morecambe and Wise went up in 2016, to commemorate the 75th anniversary of them first appearing on stage together in 1941: they went on to do more than a thousand appearances in Blackpool. Graham has done comedian Les Dawson for Lytham St Annes; fellow comedian Victoria Wood for her hometown of Bury, though she too once lived in Morecambe; and actor Cary Grant, who came from Bristol before emigrating to America. In his native Yorkshire, Graham has completed commissions of legendary Leeds United manager Don Revie; Yorkshire and England cricketer Fred Trueman, for public display in Skipton, where he lived; cricket character and Test umpire Dickie Bird, for display in his hometown of Barnsley; and furniture maker Thomas 'Mouseman' Chippendale in Otley.

Whether Cedric becomes immortalised in bronze, looking out over Morecambe Bay, only time will tell. There's talk of a part-sponsored, part crowdfunded project to make it happen. Certainly, he fits into the category of having brought joy and 'sunshine' into people's hearts, and the many charities he has helped would see it as being a fitting testimony to all his fundraising efforts.

TERN and turn-around for Morecambe

IF you want to solve a problem, and make something functional and attractive at the same time, look no further than Morecambe seafront.

What you see today is a well laid-out stone pier, jutting out into Morecambe Bay, and a coast-hugging promenade, done with artistic flair to reflect the surrounding wildlife in all its glory.

It was called the TERN Project; it reflected a simple but delightful turn for the better for the resort of Morecambe; and it turned the town back towards the Bay in a way that was tasteful. The project helped revive the run-down seafront and laid the base for better things to come. It was a statement proclaiming that Morecambe was on the way back, and by providing a backcloth, it helped inspire the idea of refurbishing the iconic Art Deco Midland Hotel; and today, the prospect of attracting the hugely-ambitious Eden Project North.

Morecambe seafront was certainly in urgent need of repair and reinvention, and the TERN Project came to the rescue. The five-mile bay seafront had been battered and breached by storms and floods for decades – and Lancaster Council had the vision to seek the perfect solution. What better than procuring grants and Government cash for coastal protection, making the new promenade into an attractive and regenerated area that was in touch with the Bay? It was seen as 'a gorgeous opportunity,' and top marks to all the bodies and individuals who helped make it happen. Function, form and flair all at the same time. William Morris would have been proud.

Cedric has always had fond memories of Morecambe, the old-style resort of his youth where he would take the train for a day out, got to go to dances with his Flookburgh pals, or go shrimping, sometimes incurring the wrath of the Heysham trawler shrimpers who guarded their side of the Bay with zeal. It saddened him to see Morecambe become a bit down at heel and, of course,

TERN-ROUND FOR MORECAMBE BAY: Statues of cormorants drying their wings form part of the TERN Project on Morecambe's Old Stone Jetty and promenade, aiming to reconnect the town with the wildlife on its doorstep in Morecambe Bay.

FLIGHT OF FANCY: A flock of seabirds in formation flight on a set of blue railings near Morecambe's Old Stone Pier. The artwork is all part of the ambitious TERN Project that helped kick-start the regeneration of Morecambe's seafront.

welcomes the schemes to help put Morecambe back on the tourist map and back in touch with the Bay.

Like everyone who visits "the other side of the Bay," as Cedric calls the Morecambe area, he appreciates the TERN Project's award-winning sculptures and art works, depicting the birdlife in the Bay. The natural setting enhances the sight of steel cormorants drying their wings on top of huge rocks, and all the other metallic seabirds placed on bollards, metal frames and seafront railings along The Stone Jetty and the promenade. Among them are gannets, gulls, razorbills, oystercatchers and swallows – all tastefully done, with a stunning background of the Bay and the Lake District hills and fells on the horizon across the water. Different people love different things and different experiences. One feedback to tourist officials was: 'I love visiting at any time, but it's best at high tide on a stormy day.' Quite elemental. Another gentler soul spoke for all by saying: 'When you reach the end of the jetty, you can almost touch the Lake District.'

Morecambe's Midland Hotel . . .
a jewel from the Thirties

AS you would expect, Cedric Robinson is not exactly an expert on art and architecture. Nor would he try to be pretentious about the subject. But he knows what he likes – and he definitely likes Morecambe's iconic Midland Hotel.

He and his wife have visited the jewel in Morecambe's hospitality crown on several occasions and he says: "It's very pleasing on the eye, lovely inside too . . . and they served up lovely afternoon teas when me and my wife have attended events there."

He's not alone in enjoying sitting on the Sun Terrace, looking across the mesmerising vistas of the Bay, while savouring the three-tiered delights of delicate finger sandwiches, Victoria sponge, fruit tartlets and luscious scones with cream and jam. Cedric smiles at the memory, and recalls: "I said to Olive: 'We could get used to this, you know.'"

All this in the relaxing atmosphere of this Art Deco classic from the 1930s, which was revived and refurbished in 2008, to once more become 'one of Britain's finest seaside hotels,' according to the *Times*.

The Midland, with its long, curving front that looks out over the Bay, is the essence of simplicity of style. Standing there in all its straight-line glory, just a short stroll from the revitalised Stone Jetty and promenade, it is testimony to a more elegant age. In its heyday, it is said to have hosted Coco Chanel, Noël Coward and Laurence Olivier. Today, it still offers a glimpse into the fashionable world of 1933 high society, albeit a world far away from the hard times being suffered by many in the neighbouring mill towns and cities that were blighted by the Great Depression of the Thirties.

The Grade II building, in the Streamline Moderne style, was restored to its former glory by the Manchester-based regeneration

JEWEL IN THE CROWN: Morecambe's 1930s Art Deco Midland Hotel, still a world-class icon of the Streamline Moderne style of architecture. Its presence on the seafront is a symbol of Morecambe's quest for a chic and relevant image for the future.

company Urban Splash, which specialises in saving Victorian buildings and utilising them for practical purposes.

Chairman Tom Bloxham, who set up Urban Splash with his architect friend, Bradford-born Jonathan Falkingham, reveals: "We had always had a fascination with the Midland Hotel, and visited many times before taking it on. What stood out most was the building's sad decline, and that was something we wanted to change.

"When it was built, it was unashamedly contemporary, and we wanted to take the same approach, restoring many of the original

Art Deco features while adding contemporary design solutions. The hotel became a symbol of renaissance for Morecambe, and as a seaside icon, tens of thousands of people are genuinely attached to it. It's great to see that the hotel is still so revered. I'm proud that we helped Morecambe's modernist masterpiece regain its rightful place as the crowning glory on the North West coast. I'm only sad we were not asked to continue our work and carry on regenerating the rest of Morecambe."

The hotel was built by the London, Midland and Scottish Railway – the old LMS – in 1933, the very year in which Cedric was born across the Bay into the hand-to-mouth existence of a typical Flookburgh family of fishermen and women. Who would have thought that Cedric would go on to be the Queen's Guide and be presented with awards as guest of honour at the Midland Hotel? As Cedric himself admits: "It's hard to take in really. Sometimes, I have to pinch myself – but I like to think I've done my bit to help put Morecambe Bay on the map for so many people, just like the Midland Hotel has done over the years. It's a bit of an irony really that the Midland and myself share the same birthday year. Unlike the hotel, I haven't had much renovation work done on myself – but we're both still going strong."

The Midland is considered to be one of the finest examples of Streamline Moderne, a breakaway type of Art Deco architecture that was 'stripped of its ornamentation.' The emphasis for Streamline was on the 'aerodynamic, pure-line concept of motion and speed,' that better reflected the more austere times of the Thirties. The building is a great illustration of the new focus on curving forms, long horizontal lines, and nautical elements. Sitting on the deck of the Bay, so to speak, all this is quite appropriate. The long, curving front of the Midland faces seaward, and looks quite majestic, almost like an ocean liner.

Other examples of the Streamline Moderne style are the Daily Express Building on the fringe of Manchester's Northern Quarter, known wickedly to journalists as 'the Black Lubianka;' the Strand

STAIRWAY TO AN ARCHITECTURAL HEAVEN: The much-admired spiral staircase that greets visitors who walk into Morecambe's world-famous Midland Hotel. The building was restored and re-crafted by Manchester regeneration company Urban Splash and is run by English Lakes Hotels.

Palace Hotel in London; Southgate and East Finchley tube stations; Regent Court in Hillsborough, Sheffield; the Coca Cola Building in Los Angeles; the Star Ferry Pier in Hong Kong; Broadway Mansions in Shanghai; and the TAV Studios in Hollywood.

The Midland is certainly in illustrious company. Its flagship design by Oliver Hill, sculpture by Eric Gill, and murals – now long gone – by Eric Ravilious, put Morecambe on the map. Gill's famous seahorses on the facade have been restored, and the Portland stone relief of Odysseus and Nausicaa was returned to its original position in the lobby. Today, the hotel stands as a symbol of Morecambe's revival plans, and no-one could be more happy about that than Cedric.

Wayne Hemingway sees a grand design for Morecambe and the Bay

IT says something that Morecambe can produce a top designer with a feel for both vintage and the cutting edge.

Wayne Hemingway, who was born and brought up in Morecambe during the early 1960s – the latter end of its heyday as a classic seaside resort – has "great affection and nothing but positivity" for his home town.

He wants the future of the 'Bay community' to be bright too, and is well aware of Queen's Guide Cedric Robinson, and his walks across what author Bill Bryson says 'may well be the most beautiful bay in Britain.' Hemingway wouldn't disagree with that and says: "Cedric is a proper jewel of the Bay, and is as much a part of the scenery as those unbeatable views to the peaks of the Lake District. He has set the scene for cross-bay walks to be what marketing folk call 'a long-term brand asset' for Morecambe and its Bay."

Hemingway made his mark with his award-winning clothes company 'Red or Dead,' before he and wife Gerardine sold it to set up 'HemingwayDesign.' As part of their operation, they run Morecambe's enormously-successful Vintage By The Sea Festival, now in its eighth year, attracting more than 40,000 visitors over the weekend event.

Hemingway sees it as "a huge party," not just an event looking back in time, but he wants more for Morecambe, to propel it into the future. "However, you have to hold out for something special, and not bite desperately at the first thing that comes along," says the 58-year-old who started out in the design world selling vintage clothes in London's Camden Market.

That 'something special' could well be the Eden Project North scheme put forward by Eden founder Sir Tim Smit. Hemingway reveals: "Tim Smit looked at the numbers attracted to our Vintage Weekend, and that gave him confidence. I think the Eden Project for Morecambe is different from other projects put forward for the prime seafront festival site over the years."

In its day, the site housed the huge Super Swimming Stadium, then Bubbles swimming pool, then the Dome Theatre and event centre. Today, with the successive demise of all these attractions, it remains as the massive open space, which is used for major festivals, including the Vintage Weekend. Hemingway tenaciously fought plans to build houses there, but backs the aspirations for Eden Project North and its five state-of-the-art, mussel-shaped bio-domes, reflecting the connection between the town and the marine life of Morecambe Bay itself.

Hemingway asks: "So why is this project different? Well, it's not privatising the space, which is Morecambe's 'crown jewel' in my opinion. It would be a public attraction and will bring in thousands of people. If it comes off, it would be going back to having a proper leisure facility for everybody. The will for it to happen is there, and the value of that space for the Eden Project, which will incorporate space for festival events too, will bring in far more than housing would ever have achieved. There are loads of places to build houses: I have no problem with them being built with a sea view on spaces available on the other side of the promenade road."

Hemingway has nothing but praise for the "fantastic refurbishment" of the iconic Midland Hotel by regeneration specialists Urban Splash, even though he opposed their subsequent plan to build houses next to it on the festival site. Hemingway says: "Everyone takes pride in the Midland. It's fabulous and gives Morecambe its glamorous focal point. Design is the most powerful thing you can do for a place, and the Midland is one of the world's greatest examples of 1930s architecture. It also attracted people of influence, like Coco Chanel, Sir Laurence Olivier and Noël Coward. The potential of Morecambe's future results from the revival of the Midland: so, congratulations to the council, Urban Splash and English Lakes Hotels, who run it well."

So how does all this stand with Hemingway's love of all things vintage? He says: "Our Vintage Festival is simply a party, dressing up and having a good time and celebrating a certain era. I don't want to take anything back in time. I want people to see how wonderful Morecambe is, with its position overlooking and connecting with the Bay. Looking back is so 'Brexit,' pretending things can be just as they were back in the 1950s and 60s. I'm unashamedly a 'Remainer,' with a positive attitude of looking forward."

Hemingway is not afraid to be political, radical and controversial, especially when the health and welfare of Morecambe is at stake. He's come a long way since those bucket and spade days when he would play on the beach, be taken to dig for lugworms by his grandfather 'Pops,' and run with the dogs on the waterfront. He says: "It was the happiest of childhoods, it was a fantastic place to grow up in, and I will always have a massive affection for the place."

In the swim, in Grange's Lido

TO some folk, it's an architectural jewel, though badly tarnished through neglect over time. To others, it's an eyesore that needs to be pulled down – and as they say north of the border: 'Ne'er the twain shall meet.'

However, the iconic Art Deco Lido on Grange-over-Sands' promenade – just a brisk, seafront walk from Cedric Robinson's home – is a Grade II building, and must be saved, in one form or another. And that's the quandary.

The 'Save Grange Lido' group want it restored to its former glory, to the condition of the days when 60,000 people a year enjoyed, and braved, the grand, 50-metre, open-air swimming pool. On the other hand, South Lakeland Council are only prepared to 'lightly refurbish' the crumbling and boarded-up buildings for commercial use.

Local MP Tim Farron at one time more than hinted that the council had pulled back from the idea of filling in the pool with landfill and with an earth topping to turn it into a garden. He claimed they were considering some form of decking over the pool area that would allow events to take place there. It would also leave open the option of it being returned to an actual lido, though that is another story, and one which provokes high passion in the Morecambe Bay area.

The council appear to now favour filling in the pool and are not convinced that an open-air pool is a viable proposition. The Save Grange Lido Community Benefit Society think otherwise. Tim Farron is on record as saying: "It's a great idea, but who's going to pay for it?" He claims that it would cost between £8 and £10 million to complete: the campaigners say it's more likely to be £1.2 million, given that the council are committed to spending £2 million in refurbishing the pool's preserved Art Deco buildings.

Now the last thing that Cedric wants is to be embroiled in a political row, but he says simply: "It was built as a lido and it

BARRED FROM USE: The rundown and decaying Grange Lido, as seen through the iron bars put up to keep out the public from the derelict pool and buildings on the promenade at Grange-over-Sands.

SPLASHING OUT, POOLSIDE: Outdoor swimmers enjoy the delights of bathing in the fresh air at Grange Lido during the pool's heyday. (Pictures supplied by Save Grange Lido).

DAYS GONE BY: A top-hatted figure makes haste to catch the pleasure boat at the old Grange Pier, near Grange Lido, on the promenade.

would be fitting if it remained as a lido. In an ideal world, a lido should be used as a lido."

When they closed the lido in 1993, a new, but ill-fated, indoor swimming pool was built just off the Allithwaite road on the way to Cedric's home. It wasn't that well used and had design flaws, causing it to be pulled down a short time later. On its site, several tastefully-designed houses and apartments were built in stone, the two roads being named in honour of Cedric and his wife – 'Cedric Walk' and 'Olive Way.' "It's a bit of an irony, all round, isn't it," says Cedric.

But if the health of Morecambe Bay – environmentally, ecologically and socially – is the big picture uppermost in the

SIGNS OF THE TIMES: In honour of their service, a street and a pathway leading to a cluster of affordable homes in Grange-over-Sands have been named 'Cedric Walk' and 'Olive Way.'

minds of coastal residents and visitors alike, the health and well-being of the individual is becoming increasingly a focus of Government, the NHS and local organisations.

That's one of the key cards played by the 'Save Grange Lido' campaigners. Just as a nationwide health movement in the 1930s led to the construction of more than 180 outdoor swimming pools, with many lidos being built around the coast, so today there is a growing move towards the concept of 'wild swimming' and the use of the remaining lidos to keep fit and healthy.

Quite recently, three of the four remaining Art Deco coastal lidos have been reopened, and Grange campaigners hope theirs is the next in line. The Saltdean Lido near Brighton has been saved with an injection of £3 million, opening in 2017, to much acclaim. Penzance's Jubilee Pool in Cornwall was restored and revived, and reopened in 2016, after £3 million was raised to make it happen. The story is the same with Plymouth's Tinside Lido. Built in 1935, it closed in 1992, was listed in 1998, then reopened in 2005 after £3.4 million was raised for its restoration. It stands adjacent to Plymouth Sound and is overlooked by Plymouth Hoe. No doubt, Sir Francis Drake would have been proud of it. Rather nice to play a game of bowls up above, while looking down on an armada of swimmers in the pool. Certainly, it has proved popular with those who use the unheated, seawater pool between the months of May and September.

'Save Grange Lido' chair Phil Bradby says: "We're trying to get Grange Lido back to life, in the same way the other three remaining Art Deco lidos have been restored. We don't want it filled with flowers. If these three lidos can do it, so can we. Grange Lido is one of the finest examples in the country, the Lake District is next door, and that's one of the most-visited places in the UK, with Windermere only eight miles from Grange."

Mr Bradby, who runs a building restoration company, and has expertise in renovation projects, adds: "Architectural plans have been drawn up already, and our business plan works on a figure of 40,000 people using it each year. That's two-thirds of the number using it in its heyday, and we think that is realistic. We reckon that if you take a 50-mile radius from Grange, there is ten times the population of Penzance. Cornwall has its tourism pull, but we have the Lakes next door, and we think that will help enormously. There is huge potential and it couldn't be a better time to do it. There's a growing emphasis on health and well-being, and outside swimming is becoming fashionable again. The Outdoor Swimming Society have given us their support, and 18,000 people signed our petition to save the lido. That's easily the biggest-ever petition in this area, and that means the communities around here support our efforts."

The campaigners want a competition-standard, 50-metre pool for summer and early autumn use, plus a 30-metre heated pool for more general use. Mr Bradby stresses that the business plan envisages putting in all the necessary pipe work and systems so that the main pool, which will have freshwater not sea water, can be heated as and when funds and demand allow.

If they win their battle, no doubt the excitement will be as great as it was on August 18th, 1932, when Lord Derby officially opened the lido, while on his way to Holker Hall for a shoot. His opening speech was made from the upper floor of the central building, high above the pool, and he added: "If anyone thinks I am going to dive in from here, they will be very disappointed."

Long before the Lido was built, Grange was on the map. The coast-hugging railway was the catalyst in the mid-19th century, and the 'branding' of the town as 'the Torquay of the North' helped establish Grange as a major Morecambe Bay magnet in Edwardian times. It still has a genteel, health spa feel, with its promenade and gardens, but is far more vibrant than it first appears. In addition, the panoramic view of the Bay from Hampsfell, above the town, is magnificent. Cedric has great affection for his 'home town' of 55 years and that affection is reciprocated. Everyone knows Cedric in Grange.

Arnside, where mud turned to 'gold'

CEDRIC'S name was once mud in the little town of Arnside . . . then the mud turned to 'gold.'

When Cedric changed the start of his cross-bay walks from Hest Bank to setting off from Arnside instead, hundreds of walkers suddenly descended on the picturesque, seaside town. That led to car parking pressures, but also to tills ringing in shops, cafes, pubs, the fish and chip shop, hotels and B&Bs. That, in turn, led to a seachange in attitudes towards Cedric too. Today, there are no empty shops in this pleasant and unassuming town that looks out on the gently-flowing River Kent and its estuary.

As Cedric himself says: "The cross-bay walkers helped put Arnside – and Morecambe Bay in general – on the map, and that has attracted more visitors. The town has always been an attractive place, looking out on the Kent and the low railway viaduct. I love Arnside. There's something quite special about the place, and people who are introduced to the town come back again and again, not only to do the walk. I'm even told that some have been spurred into buying a house there, with other folk planning a move in the future."

He adds: "People who come by train for the walks can get off in

KNOTT WITHSTANDING: The stunning panoramic view from Arnside Knott, taking in the railway viaduct over the Kent Estuary, with the Lakeland hills and fells on the far horizon.

Arnside, then return from Kents Bank. For those coming by car, parking has to be accommodated. But with a bit of common sense all round, it's nothing that can't be sorted. The walking brigade tend not to be loud, aggressive or problematical – and it's only twice a fortnight in the season."

As Cedric outlines, the attractions of Arnside are there for all to see and to explore, especially if people stay for a couple of days or so. It's part of the Arnside and Silverdale Area of Outstanding Natural Beauty and is one of the remaining strongholds of the red squirrel. There are alpine plants, rare butterflies and orchids, limestone pavements and scars. The tidal bore up the River Kent channel always engenders excitement, as the surge of the incoming tide is funnelled against the fresh water flowing out and the resistance of the sands. Cedric often warns folk of the power of the tides, adding: "The water can come in faster than a galloping horse."

Viewing the estuary from the 520ft-high Arnside Knott, the hill that rises up behind the town, is stunning. In front of you, the Kent channel bends and switches across the estuary, the water glistening in the sunshine, and the Lake District mountains and fells standing as a backcloth on the horizon.

Finally, a true and salutary tale from Cedric. He relates: "One family who had been on a walk decided to revisit Arnside some time much later. Initially, they had parked on the big, low car park adjacent to the railway viaduct when there was a low tide. They did the same when they returned, not realising that later on that day, there would be a very high tide, which floods on to the car park. Off they went by train towards Barrow and the west coast to Whitehaven. Hours later, as they were returning across the railway viaduct, one of their children shouted: 'The water has come up and our car is floating!' The family had to wait for the tide to ebb away to reach the vehicle. Amazingly, it started up straight away and off they drove home.

"A week or so later, they wrote me a letter telling me that every time they went up or down an incline, the sound of running water came from the chassis. They signed off saying that they should have approached me for my advice. I wrote back and told them: 'The only advice I can give you is to sell the car as quickly as possible!'"

Prevent Breast Cancer is the only UK breast cancer charity funding groundbreaking research solely aimed at preventing the disease for future generations.

Our research will one day bring about a world where breast cancer is preventable, thousands of lives are saved from ever experiencing this terrible disease. Breast cancer is the most common cancer in the UK.

At Prevent Breast Cancer, we're passionate about stopping the disease before it starts. We promote healthier lifestyles and early diagnosis. We also collaborate with others to influence change in breast cancer services.

Walking across Morecambe Bay Sands with Cedric Robinson MBE has been an annual highlight for many of our supporters, with some returning each year to take part with friends and family. Getting the chance to see the beauty of the Bay and experience the feeling of sand under your feet whilst walking through a river channel is something which can't be beaten!

So, thank you Cedric for the support you have given us and for planning such brilliant routes across the Bay. Over the last 8 years you have helped us to raise over £20,000!

Thanks also to the author and publisher for including us in this book. I'm really grateful that we have been given the chance to thank Cedric for everything he's done, not only for Prevent Breast Cancer, but for all the other charities and organisations that have benefited from his expertise during the last 55 years.

Caroline Bennison,
Community Fundraiser.
Prevent Breast Cancer

Cedric Robinson - Queen's Guide to Morecambe Bay

Grange Over Sands Town Council 2015

Faith, hope and charity . . .
big-style and Bay-style

CEDRIC and myself sat by his roaring open fire in Guide's Farm, captivated by its flames and its heat. Just sitting there contented and in silence, his wife Olive yet to come down from the bedroom.

The silence was broken by Ced as he said softly: "I know why you're doing this book you know. It's certainly not for the money, is it?" We both laughed a little. "No," I said. "It's for you and Olive. I think you deserve a thank-you . . . before we both drown out there." Cedric likes black humour, and he laughed again. Then he added gently: "Aye, but it's more than that, isn't it? It's for your brother."

He was right, of course. He usually is. I nodded, holding back a bit of a tear that was welling up. Ced continued: "He was a lovely chap, and he loved coming every year – and you loved being with him. I could always see that." Graham, my older brother, had learning difficulties and whenever he came on a cross-bay walk with me, Cedric made a real fuss of him, making him feel like part of the family. I loved that and I've always been grateful to Cedric and Olive for ensuring that Graham had a great day out and felt part of the fraternity.

Ced greeted him at Arnside, talked to him as we strode up front on our way to White Creek and the sands. There, we always had to take a photo of Ced with his arm round Graham's shoulders. Later on, like everyone, Graham was excited going through the River Kent channel. He gripped my hand tightly as we waded

AND DID THOSE FEET? Cedric's footsteps in the sand have been cast in bronze and placed for all to see in a public garden area near to 'Cedric Walk,' named after the record-holding Queen's Guide to the Sands. (Picture by Mary T Holland)

across to the other side, then chatted to everyone, as though he was fine about the whole thing. At the end of each walk, Cedric insisted on giving him a signed certificate, which went up back at his home in Bradford. And I was happy when Olive said each and every time: "He's a love, isn't he?" He was a love, right up to the end, when he died of lung cancer, never having smoked a cigarette in his life. I always suspected that cafes, top decks of buses, the workmen's hut where he sat down for his 'dinner' were to blame, the atmosphere being thick as fog, before the smoking bans came in. You'll notice he always had his 'dinner' midday, after a morning's work as a labourer to the local parks' gardeners. People don't have 'lunch' in Bradford.

I tell all this, not only to inform you of the considerate nature of Cedric and Olive, but also because that's why 10,000 people do this walk every year – to raise money for people like my brother, and for charities that help look after them. Graham was lucky to have loving people around him, to give him the safety net and the warmth needed to live a meaningful life. Not everyone is so lucky.

That's why Cedric's trusted 'walks' wingman' John Holland, from Chorley, helped collect the testimony of many of the charities that have benefited from the fundraising, cross-bay walks. John and myself have interspersed them throughout the book. No more need be said: they speak for themselves.

We really can't thank Cedric Robinson MBE enough for his expertise and guidance when organising our walks across the Bay. His knowledge of the area and conditions was excellent,  allowing us to plan successful walks. His kind and approachable nature made organising the walks a pleasure. Even during the times when the conditions were against us and we had to postpone them, Cedric always gave really detailed information on the conditions of the Bay, and the commitment he and his team showed in trying to make the walks happen, spending full days on the sands the day before is a true testament to how much he wanted to help.

As a local charity, the funds we have raised from the cross-bay walks has been vital and without Cedric we simply wouldn't have been able to raise the money we have. He will certainly be missed, and we would like to say a huge thank you from everyone at Age UK Lancashire for his support and guidance.

David Ward,
Promotions and Fundraising Manager,
Age UK Lancashire

Morecambe Bay, set against the stunning Lake District skyline, is a thing of beauty and a jewel in the footprint served by CancerCare.

The cross-bay walk, a regular feature in our fundraising calendar, is very special to us as its route links together the wide geography covered by our charity.

Having walked with you for the first time many years ago, I still recall the wonder of the experience and the warmth of your character. Little did I think that one day I would end up leading a local cancer support charity that has for more than 10 years organised a fundraising cross-bay walk!

We are so grateful for your incredible support for our charity over the years by hosting many of these cross-bay walks and guiding CancerCare supporters safely across the Bay, all the while passing on your unmatched knowledge of the sands.

As a result of these fantastic walks, more than £170,000 has been raised to provide specialist therapy and support services to families affected by cancer across North Lancashire and South Cumbria.

Many thanks from all the staff, volunteers and, most of all, the clients of CancerCare who have been helped by the remarkable funds raised through your cross-bay walks!

**Neil Townsend,
Chief Executive,
CancerCare.**

On behalf of all of us here at Heartbeat, we would like to thank Cedric Robinson MBE for all his help and support during the past few years.

As a charity we are relatively new at taking walkers across the Bay. However we always felt so very welcome.

Cedric has always been very accommodating with dates and really tried to find a suitable route across the sands during bad weather. This has enabled Heartbeat to raise much-needed funds, whilst at the same time giving our volunteers and fundraisers the opportunity to enjoy the wonders of Morecambe Bay.

A gentleman and a true legend.

We wish you well in your new role, Cedric and maybe even find some time to put those feet up and relax.

**Lisa Riding,
Heartbeat Senior Fundraiser.**

Cedric Robinson MBE has been a long-time supporter of the University of Central Lancashire (UCLan). We were enormously privileged when he accepted an Honorary Fellowship from us back in 1989. Since then, he and his wife Olive have regularly attended our graduation ceremonies, meaning he has inspired and been a role model to our students for almost 30 years.

Throughout the past three decades, Cedric has also been a regular attendee at a range of University events, including the UCLan Honorary Fellows' dinner. He has also been an inspirational guest speaker at the Harris Alumni Reunion Lunch.

As the Queen's Guide to the Sands of Morecambe Bay, Cedric has volunteered his services to leading many UCLan fundraising walks. During eight walks, from Arnside to Grange-over-Sands, he has guided more than 2,500 walkers across Morecambe Bay. These walks helped raise nearly £50,000 for various North West charities, including our Harris Bursary Fund, which supports students in financial hardship who are in danger of dropping out of their studies.

Rachel Atkinson,
Corporate Communications Officer.
University of Central Lancashire

Summary of some awards, honours and recognition made to Cedric Robinson for service as the Queen's Guide to the Sands.

***

1985 Morecambe Bay Sands won the prize for the Television Film of the Year, and the United Nations Environment Programme Silver Medal. Both awards were won in the second European Environmental Film Festival held in Rotterdam, on the theme 'Man and Water'.

***

1989 Awarded Hon Fellowship, Master of Science and Technology by the then Lancashire Polytechnic, now the University of Central Lancashire (UCLan).

***

Lancaster University. Cedric Robinson has been duly admitted to the Degree of Master of Science. 11th July 1996.

***

1998 Bernard Gooch **Cumbria Personality of the Year Award**, for Services to Tourism.

***

MBE – 12th June 1999

Elizabeth the Second, by the Grace of God of the United Kingdom of Great Britain and Northern Ireland and of Her other Realms and Territories, Queen, Head of the Commonwealth, Defender of the Faith and Sovereign of the Most Excellent Order of the British Empire to our trusty and well beloved Cedric Robinson Esquire.

***

HONOUR FOR A GUIDING HAND: Cedric and his wife
Olive hold the MBE which was awarded to him by the Queen
in a special ceremony at Buckingham Palace.

Cumbria Tourist Board, Lakeland Book of the Year Awards 1999 "Sand Pilot of Morecambe Bay."

***

Grange-over-Sands Town Council Civic Award 2001.

In Recognition and Sincere Appreciation for the Services Rendered to the Community Life and Wellbeing of the Citizens of Grange-over-Sands.

***

In 2002 the Morecambe Bay Partnership granted Honorary Life Membership to Cedric and Olive Robinson.

***

2003, The Golden Eagle Award of the Outdoor Writers Guild was presented for services to the community.

***

2007 Moorhouse's Brewery brew a beer in Cedric's honour, marking the outstanding contribution he has made to Grange-over-Sands during his long career as the Queen's Guide.

***

Cumbria Tourism and Hunter Davis Lakeland Book of the Year Awards 2008. (*Between the Tides.*)

***

Lancashire and Blackpool Tourist Board, Tourism Awards 2008/09 Tourism Ambassador, for leading walks across Morecambe Bay, and Best Tourism Experience of the Year.

***

Morecambe Town Council 2013, the Council unanimously agreed to honour Cedric Robinson MBE, *as a great ambassador for Morecambe over the last 50 years which has helped to promote the Town in particular its unique asset of Morecambe Bay.*

***

2013: The University of Cumbria. *Awarded an Honorary Fellowship in recognition of his outstanding service to the Community and significant contribution to supporting charitable causes, both locally and globally.*

***

Lancaster and Morecambe Council Sunshine Awards, Ambassador 2013.

***

2013: The Royal National Lifeboat Institution award for his 50 years of dedication and commitment to Morecambe Sands, safely escorting RNLI and many other charity fundraisers on the Cross Bay Walks.

***

2014: City of Lancaster, confers the **Freedom of the City of Lancaster**, in recognition of his role as Queen's Guide to the Sands.

***

2015: Cumbria High Sheriffs Award. This award was made by The High Sheriff of Cumbria, *in recognition of the great and valuable service to the community.*

***

GLORIOUS REFLECTIONS:
As the sun sets on Cedric's record
term as Guide to the Morecambe Bay
Sands, he has much to be proud of.
(Picture by Paul Nickson)

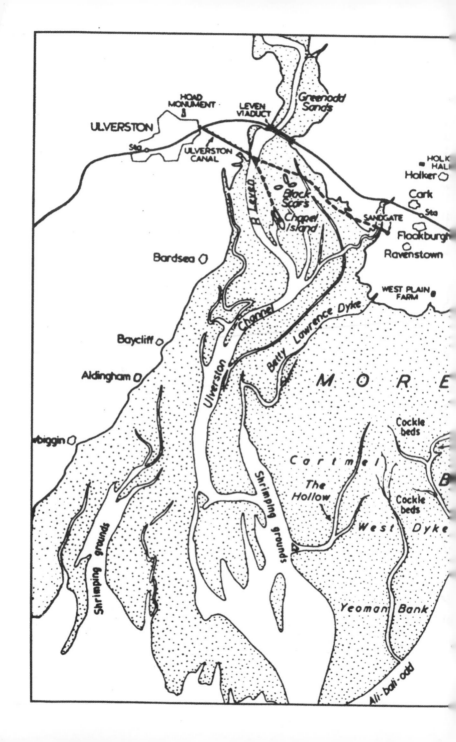